Kids

and

Cars

A Parent's Survival Guide for Family Travel

Ellyce Field & Susan Shlom

Library of Congress Cataloging-in-Publication Data

Field, Ellyce, 1951-
    Kids and cars.

    Includes index.
    1. Travel. 2. Games for travelers. I. Shlom,
Susan, 1950-   . II. Title.
G151.F46 1988   910'.2'02   87-60793
ISBN 0-937603-00-7 (pbk.)

Cover design by Victoria Cavalier

Manufactured in the United States of America.

9 8 7 5 4 3 2

First Edition

ADDRESS FOR ORDERS: Melius & Peterson Publishing, Inc.
                    P.O. Box 925
                    Aberdeen, SD 57401
                    (605) 226-0488

To Steve
and Jordan and Andrew and Garrett

To Gordon
and Samara and Adam

TABLE OF CONTENTS

INTRODUCTION

As parents, we approach family travel with mixed feelings. We want to travel with our kids but it's often a frustrating experience. If they aren't crying and fighting, then they're tired or hungry, or have to use the bathroom. Let's face it, we could go faster and farther without them!

Like you, we've spent hours cramped in the car's backseat playing cards with a bored seven-year-old. We've been awakened at 5:00 a.m., still sore from carrying baby and his equipment. We've fallen victim to the "just this once" argument and bought unnecessary treats for a frantic four-year-old. We've even spent two gloriously sunny days in a small hotel room with a sick child.

In any case, family car travel is inevitable. Even if you have no desire to take a month's drive across country, you certainly will be lured into visiting grandparents, siblings or friends who may not live close by. Your trip may be as long as a five-hour drive across the state or as short as an hour through the city.

We learned through extensive travel experiences that the tears and tension of family travel are greatly offset by the benefits. How else can you relive your childhood? Family travel offers children an enriching experience; they will grow and learn. Your family will build shared experiences and rich memories.

We wrote this book to help organize families who travel. Through trial and error, and the practical suggestions of over 200 parents who responded to a survey, we compiled our practical, "how to" book.

Kids and Cars: A Parent Survival Guide for Family Travel is a book we wish we had owned on our early trips. It would have helped us plan more carefully, be better prepared, have more fun and best of all, provided us with keepsake pages to permanently record precious memories.

Happy Travels,

Ellyce Field
Susan Shlom

HOW TO USE THIS BOOK

Kids and Cars is a family travel guide, a family keepsake and an activity book.

- **Read this book before you travel with your children.**
  The checklists and questions offer you a chance to plan ahead, sort out your expectations, pack creatively, tour with a relaxed attitude and return home intact.

- **Take this book along on your trip.**
  Slip it into a travel bag that will be at arm's reach. Use it as needed for tips, advice and activities.

- **Fill in Keepsake and Daily Log Pages.**
  These pages become a permanent collection of your family's ideas and travel activities. Coloring pages are provided for children too young to write.

  Bring pens, pencils, crayons, paper and tape so everyone can participate while you travel.

- **Reserve a Special Spot in your home for Kids and Cars.**
  Thumb through the Keepsake and Daily Log Pages often. You'll never forget your family travel adventures.

NOTE: Throughout the book you'll notice we often use pronouns "he" and "him." This is only to simplify our language and doesn't indicate a preference for boys. (Although with four sons between us, we do like them!) We also refer to accomodations as "hotel," while realizing that motels, cabins, camp grounds and relatives' homes are all viable places to stay.

HOW TO USE THE ILLUSTRATIONS IN THIS BOOK

Meet Traveling Timothy. He's a spunky little bird who loves to travel. His hobby appears to be arranging silly predicaments for himself.

If you're a keen observer, you'll notice that Traveling Timothy pops up in almost every illustration.

You can have fun with your children using the illustrations in this book as the basis for activities.

Invite your children to:

_____ search for Traveling Timothy in his many predicaments

_____ invent new adventures for Timothy

_____ count the number of cars in the titles

_____ identify the objects in the titles

_____ color in the illustrations

_____ create stories about the illustrations

Getting Ready

PLANNING

Most of us have memories of the trips we took with our families. The crazy things we did; the great places we visited. Images trapped forever in instamatic shots. Mom and Jordan standing like soldiers in front of the White House, Doug and Nancy smiling next to their sand castle at the beach, Missy and Paul horsing around the Grand Tetons.

Layer upon layer of summer, winter and in-between trips helped us grow and broaden our experience.

Now it's time for us to travel with our own children.

It may start with that invitation from Aunt Liz, asking the family to come to Philadelphia for Uncle Alan's 50th birthday party . . . or the glossy brochure from a family camp in Vermont . . . or your neighbor's description of the Six Flags Park only two hours from home.

You can't postpone any longer. You're about to embark on your next family vacation.

Decisions

WHO'S GOING?

Why take the kids?

- Kids broaden our travel horizons.
  You have a secret passion for wax museums, zoos, and caves. Now you have an excuse to go.

- Kids encourage us to take it easy.
  Your child's need for his 3:00 p.m. nap will check your insane urge to visit every museum, historic site, and shopping plaza. (You probably need a nap too!)

- Kids derive spontaneous pleasure.
  You've planned a stimulating and adventurous day at a breathtaking National Park. Your child squeals with delight at an iguana in the sand, and claims the ice cream here is the best in the world. You too begin to smile at these small miracles! (Sometimes even ignoring the scenic wonder.)

- Kids see things from a unique viewpoint.
  We will always remember our four-year-old at Disneyland asking in an urgent tone, "Is that the real Mickey Mouse?" (We enthusiastically answered "Yes!," feeling like we just met a celebrity.)

- Kids are young for a short time.
  Grab them while you've got them! (Ask any middle-aged parent whose children are grown.)

Should everyone go?

- Some families take one child on a trip to celebrate a special birthday. The other children know they too will have their turn.
- One couple took the baby on a cruise, leaving the older children home with Grandma and Grandpa. A special weekend trip for the older children was planned for a later date.
- Babies are sometimes left at home so parents may concentrate on special time with older children.
- In some families, only one parent has time off work. The benefits of a father-child trip are great. The travelers may even return to a wonderfully relaxed Mom.
- Single parents know that travel with children doesn't cease just because one adult is available.

Why take Baby?

- He'll never remember Niagara Falls, and an amusement park maybe a ho-hum affair. Even a circus may provoke a nap. Yet babies are seen everywhere.
- Babies are portable. They travel well and sightsee easily in stroller or backpack.
- Babies don't say they're bored. If the antique car show is not to their liking, they just nod off or concentrate on the people.
- Babies don't wander off into the crowd. Though you have to tote or push them, at least you always know where they are.
- Babies are fun to enjoy away from the distraction of daily chores.

Who could stay with the kids?

A grandparent or familiar relative is the ideal person to stay with children not going on the trip.

HINT: To insure success, provide backup support: friends who'll take the child for the day, cleaning help, or daytime or evening babysitters. We once hired a baby nurse who stayed overnight and helped a willing, but overwhelmed Grandma and Grandpa care for one-year-old twins.

Alternative Caregivers

- Friends Who Have Children.
  Create a trade-off. Practice by having the child sleep over prior to the trip.
- Someone Else's Grandma.
  Staying with children of vacationing parents is a profession for many senior citizens.
- College Student.
  Ask friends and neighbors to suggest a student majoring in early childhood education or nursing. Or call your local college's placement service.
- Agency Babysitter.
  Most cities have yellow page listings under infant and child care.
- Nursery School or Day Care Teacher.
  Call your local nursery school or day care center to ask for possible referrals.

Rules to Remember

1. You must feel comfortable leaving your child with the caregivers. If you're distracted by concern for a child at home, you won't have much fun on vacation.
2. Check references thoroughly.
3. Leave children with someone they know and enjoy. Have your caregiver over several times before the trip.
4. Be certain the caregiver is prepared to play with and enjoy the child. Just being physically there isn't enough.
5. Discuss duties and expectations. Is the caregiver required to make all meals and do laundry? Does the caregiver have permission to take the children on an outing?
6. Be explicit about wages.
7. Leave precise instructions about visitors to the home, especially the caregiver's friends. (You haven't checked their references.)
8. Ask a neighbor, friend or relative to check in or drop by a few times. Be certain he can reach you if he suspects a problem.
9. Leave the phone number and address of your destination. Also leave your license plate number and a description of your car. In case of an emergency, the State Police could find you mid-route.
10. Leave your caregiver a medical release form authorizing emergency medical treatment for minors.

EMERGENCY MEDICAL TREATMENT AUTHORIZATION

If you are traveling with a babysitter who is a minor, you should obtain a power of attorney from the parents giving you the right to approve emergency medical treatment.

If your child is left with grandparents or another caregiver, you should also authorize emergency medical care.

Remember to obtain home and work numbers for each parent of your babysitter, or other young travel helpers. Be certain to leave numbers where you may be reached while on vacation.

THE AUTHORS ARE NOT ATTORNEYS AND DO NOT REPRESENT THE FOLLOWING FORM TO MEET THE LEGAL REQUIREMENTS OF ANY SPECIFIC STATE OR PROVINCE, BUT SUGGEST THAT IT MAY BE SUFFICIENT.

POWER OF ATTORNEY

The undersigned are parents of _____.

We hereby give power of attorney to _____

to consent on our behalf to any emergency medical treatment for our child _____. This may be revoked

orally or in writing at any time by either parent.

father: _____

mother: _____

Subscribed and sworn to before me,

_____

Notary Public, County of _____, State of _____

my commission expires _____

dated _____

Who else could we bring?

Many parents told us they always travel with an extra adult to help them with their children. Extra hands simplify your travel by dividing up caretaking responsibilities and often allow Mom and Dad some vacation time alone. Be careful to have open communication with your "guest." Go over what he is expected to contribute toward expenses, as well as his duties. For minors, remember to bring a parental consent form authorizing emergency medical care.

- A Babysitter
  If your car is roomy enough, and you don't mind the extra responsibility, bring along the kids' favorite babysitter. Carefully outline your needs and expectations. We know of an unfortunate 16-year-old who accompanied a family with three children to Florida. She thought she'd be lying in the sun every day but ended up only babysitting, and very upset.

- A Grandparent
  A lot of families enjoy traveling with Grandma or Grandpa. For many widowed grandparents, a chance to travel with their children and grandchildren is an opportunity to go somewhere they wouldn't go alone. Be sure to respect Grandma's need for privacy. Don't expect her to stay with the kids all the time! Communicate your own needs too.

- Another Relative
  Explore your family circle. There might be a wonderful travel companion available. A cousin, uncle, or niece may welcome the opportunity to travel with your family. Be sure to fully discuss how he's expected to help.

- Another Family
  Many families enjoy traveling with another family. Preserve your friendship by discussing all the details of the trip beforehand. Who will pay for gas? food? entertainment? Will you travel together in one car or as a car caravan? We like car caravans. You can switch the kids midway. They'll take the noisy four-year-olds and you'll take the quiet twelve-year-olds. Avoid traveling with families who insist on dictating the terms of the trip.

What if Grandma and Grandpa want to take the kids on vacation?

So Grandma and Grandpa want to take the grandkids to the Grand Canyon! Not every grandparent is inclined to take grandchildren on trips, but some insist this is an adventure they'd never pass up. One Grandmother told us, "I feel young when I see things through the eyes of children. Traveling with my grandchildren really lets me get to know them."

Preliminaries

Grandparents:
1. Check with Mom and Dad to see if they really feel comfortable letting Andrew go without them.
2. Pick a trip of only a few days.
3. Choose a site that interests both you and your grandchildren.
4. Don't overexert yourself or overestimate your stamina.

Benefits
1. Terrific memories are created for the grandchild to cherish, while cementing the relationship between grandparent and grandchild.
2. The grandchild receives extra special attention that parents don't always have time for.
3. Grandparents can give a gift that is enduring, rather than a toy or gadget that will be outgrown or discarded.
4. Grandparents are able to share their values and life views, tell stories about their childhood and about the children's parents.
5. Above all, Mom and Dad are offered a break from parenting for a few days. This is a most refreshing and priceless gift!

Hazards
1. Kids get sick. Be certain to take a medical release form signed by the parents, and the necessary health insurance forms. Know what the parents do for fever, stuffed nose, or any other common problems or allergies.
2. If you take siblings or cousins, there may be squabbles for grandma's attention.
3. Sometimes grandparents just can't participate in all available activities. One grandma found herself on a wild amusement park ride screaming along with her five-year old grandson. After the ride she wobbled off and with a half smile announced, "I'm 69 years old; it's about time I learned how to say 'no.' "
4. Discipline can be a problem when grandparents are overindulgent. An afternoon outing may not be a problem, but a three-day trip may be horrible if the child tries to get everything he wants.
5. Traveling with children can be tiring. Plan a rest when you return home.

Where Should We Go?

Some families enjoy a relaxing, playful week at the shore. Others like driving up and down coasts and through cities, staying overnight in many spots.

What's the right type of trip for you?

Skim through guidebooks and brochures while asking yourself:

1. What does each destination offer?
2. Is there something fun for each child?
3. Will I find something of interest?
4. What will the weather be like?
5. How much driving will we do?
6. How long can we stay?
7. Will the kids miss school?
8. Will we miss important events at home?
9. Where will we stay?
10. Are the projected costs within our budget?

Where Should We Stay?

Hopefully, travel takes us from our familiar, cozy beds to a comfortable home away from home.

Exactly how much room do we need to be comfortable?

What types of services do we require?

How important is our hotel's location?

Determine your needs:

_____ kitchenette

_____ room service

_____ several restaurants in
building

_____ free parking

_____ supervised parking

_____ indoor pool

_____ tennis courts

_____ game room

_____ children's activities

_____ other:

_____ adjoining rooms

_____ beds for each family
member

_____ luxury accomodations

_____ privacy

_____ other:

_____ nearby coffee shop

_____ meals included in
package price

_____ other:

_____ indoor garage

_____ other:

_____ outdoor pool

_____ golf course

_____ health club

_____ gift shop

_____ other:

_____ one large room

_____ cribs available

_____ spartan but clean

_____ togetherness

_____ other:

Walking distance to:

_____ park

_____ playground

_____ public transportation

_____ main attractions

_____ other:

_____ beach

_____ shopping

_____ friends or family

_____ restaurants

_____ other:

ROOM RESERVATION CALLING GUIDE

When you call for reservations ask lots of questions. Just asking for room rates isn't enough.

- Are there special rates for children, seniors, teachers, or other professionals?
- Are children free under a certain age?
- Are there special rates for weekend packages?
- Are there special off-season rates?
- What kind of rooms are available? Kitchenettes, sitting rooms, adjoining rooms, or suites?
- What sort of beds are available? Double, queen size, king size, cribs, cots or roll-away beds?
- Are there extra charges for cots or cribs?
- Do cribs adhere to present safety standards?
- Do cribs come equipped with bumper pads and sheets?
- Is my room guaranteed? How do I guarantee it? After a certain evening hour, usually 6:00 p.m., your room may be forfeited, unless you have paid for it ahead of time. If you've paid ahead, but do not use the room, you are still charged for it. Ask how far in advance must you cancel to receive your money back.
- Is there room service?
- What are the restaurant or coffee shop hours?
- Is there a buffet? Do children eat free in any restaurants?
- Is babysitting available?
- What activities are available? Indoor/outdoor pool with a lifeguard, sauna, tennis court, game room, health club or children's activities?
- What are the parking arrangements?

HINTS:
- If you will arrive late with sleeping children, call ahead so the room is arranged. Often cribs or cots aren't delivered until after check-in.
- If you plan to pick a hotel as you drive, use a reputable guidebook. At an early afternoon stop, call ahead for a room.
- If you'll have a kitchenette, ask what is provided.
- Some hotels provide a small refrigerator for your room upon request. Ask if there will be a charge.
- Extra money spent on larger accomodations (adjoining rooms, sitting room, kitchenette) may mean a real vacation for parents.
- If traveling in peak season, camp grounds and hotels should be booked months in advance.

What if we're staying with relatives or friends?

Be Direct.

Ask them what sort of accomodations they've planned for you. Tell them what you'll require. Offer to rent equipment or bring your own. Their one-year-old may have been a petite, docile baby who slept well in a port-a-crib. Your one-year-old may be a robust, active baby who requires the sturdiness of a standard crib.

If your ten-month-old refuses to sleep when he can see you, and your relative plans to put the crib right next to your bed, be creative. There must be someplace else for the crib, or some sort of partition you can create.

Be Honest.

If you . . . .
    . . . . crave privacy
    . . . . hate to see another human before your morning coffee
    . . . . let baby cry himself to sleep in the middle of the night . . . .
you may have difficulty rooming with others.

Be Comfortable.

Great Aunt Marilyn and even Grandpa and Grandma may have amnesia concerning the activities of a toddler and a five-year-old. Are they prepared for a sticky kitchen floor, noisy tantrums, potty time, and the table manners of two monkeys? Do they have a swing set, or toys, or the type of food two-year-olds enjoy?

Many parents feel more comfortable staying with families who have young children. Of course, this isn't always possible.

If you'll be staying with Aunt Marilyn or Grandma and Grandpa, send them a friendly letter outlining your needs. Explain how to minimally child-proof their home (moving breakable items off reachable shelves, checking hanging cords and exposed outlets), and give them a list of suggested food and snacks the kids will enjoy.

Be Sensitive.

• Recognize and enforce your hosts' rules even if they are different from your own:
No eating outside the kitchen
No jumping on the furniture
Shoes off at the door
• Prepare your children for your hosts' different rules and expectations:
"Grandma and Grandpa aren't used to a lot of noisy fighting."
"Aunt Marilyn lives in a top-floor apartment, so don't jump or walk heavily."

Be Prepared.

• Are there enough beds for the entire family?
• Will anyone mind sleeping on a couch, air mattress or sleeping bag?
• Will your schedule fit into your hosts' routine?
• Are you sure the invitation to stay was genuinely offered?
• Can you live with their chaos, noise and disorder? Can they live with yours?
• Have you truthfully described your children's needs and habits?
• Are your children going to cooperate enough for you to have a relaxed stay?
• Did you bring an adequate thank you gift?

THE HOUSE GUEST PLEDGE

Repeat after us. "We solemnly swear to . . . .

1. Never stay longer than stated before we arrived.

2. Always help with meals and dishes.

3. Never leave our things lying around.

4. Be sensitive to the household routine and our hosts' bedtimes.

5. Treat our hosts to a meal or special outing.

6. Offer to strip the bedsheets and wash them before we leave.

7. Extend an invitation for our hosts to stay in our home."

How Much Money Can We Spend?

Budget Expenses:

Deciding on a budget is essential. Consider all possible expenses to determine an affordable trip.

Potential expenses:

_____ car: gas, oil, tolls, parking
_____ clothes and equipment
_____ car ride: toys, games, books, food
_____ meals
_____ accomodations
_____ activities: admissions, rentals
_____ souvenirs and presents
_____ babysitter, caregiver
_____ other:

How to Cut Costs:

1. Stay with relatives or friends.
2. Stay in budget hotels or camp grounds.
3. Eat certain meals (like breakfast) in your room.
4. For summer resort-town travel, buy food from local groceries and have picnic meals.
5. Brown bag meals to theme parks where food is costly.
6. Consider "one-price family package" vacations.

Include Children:

Children can also be included in financial planning. One inventive Mom asked her pre-teen children to plan the family trip, after giving them a budget. The result was a well researched family vacation.

Prior to your trip, decide how much each child may spend on souvenirs, extra treats or video-game arcades. This makes each child responsible for his own expenditures and helps eliminate the constant tension of a child pleading, "Can I have this one and this one and this one . . . . pleeease!"

Children like knowing the price of items. For a learning experience, keep a log of travel expenses.

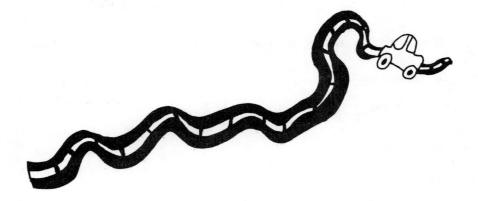

How Long Can We Travel?

The number of days you travel depends on your schedule, amount of vacation time and desire. We recommend taking short trips at first to build up to the big trip.

- **Active toddlers are better on short car rides.**

Several parents vowed never to take an active toddler on a vacation again. Long car rides are often a challenge. Try a short car trip. If a long trip is unavoidable, travel during naps or nighttime. Look for a hotel or motel with a park or indoor shopping center nearby. Stop for run-around breaks regularly. Plan to take longer getting to your destination.

- **Consider a trip to a nearby hotel or resort.**

Getting away doesn't necessarily mean far away. Many of us live within an hour's drive of a hotel or resort that offers family activities.

- **Stay long enough to settle in.**

A family vacation shouldn't be rushed. Everyone may be restless the first few nights in an unfamiliar bed, but the third and fourth nights are much better. Explore the sights at a leisurely pace.

- **Veteran travelers suggest arriving home one day early.**

Everyone needs to relax before returning to routines. Adults need to change gears before returning to work. Someone has to unload the car, unpack, reorganize and attack the mountain of laundry.

Children need time to readjust before returning to school, day camp, or child care.

ACTIVITY PAGE

Enrich your child's appreciation of your destination and increase his anticipation and excitement.

1. Talk about the trip as a family; be open about concerns too. "I'm wondering if you kids could handle a two-day car drive to Florida? What do you think?

2. Present maps and guidebooks to older children. Ask them to research and select places of interest.

3. Show younger children pictures of their destination. Ask them to make up a story about one of the pictures.

4. Show children photographs of the people you'll be visiting to familiarize them with names and places. Share a story about each person.

5. For trips to famous historical sites, visit the library for books about historic events and famous people.

6. For trips to natural wonders, show pictures or pamphlets. Ask everyone to imagine how this natural wonder was created. Pretend to be scientists and give a scientific explanation.

7. If a city is your destination, ask children to write a story entitled "Our Amazing Adventure in Chicago" (New York, Atlanta, Los Angeles . . . . etc.). Encourage them to daydream and add all sorts of imaginative events.

8. Young children may draw the seashore, the city, the National Park, etc.

9. Invite older children to help select hotels from a guidebook.

10. Show everyone the map, and the route you'll be taking. Explain how long it takes to get from here to there.

KEEPSAKE PAGE

Which answers best describe why you want to take a family vacation? Have each family member participate.

Compare your answers; be ready for some surprises.

We're taking a trip in order to . . .

- relax
- get away from it all
- have a break in routine
- visit relatives/friends
- sightsee
- have a family adventure
- spend time together
- have fun
- enjoy sports
- visit a special place of interest
- others:

Expectations

EXPECTATIONS

One of the greatest sources of tension and tears on a family trip stems from expectations either not fully discussed or not realistic. We've learned from experience to anticipate the problems before they arise and hash them out before we leave.

CHILD CARE

Who's Taking Care of Whom?
When two parents take two children on a trip, are they equals sharing child care, or will Mom assume the greater responsibilities since she often does at home? Who will wake up to feed Baby? Take Michael to the potty? Change Jeffrey's diaper? Pick your jobs:

_____ Baby Bouncer
Always on call. Wakes up at crack of dawn. Feeds Baby anywhere, anytime. Dresses, bathes, changes, distracts and soothes Baby. Left shoulder of all outfits has permanent spit-up stains.

_____ Shower Sergeant
Marches dirty children into shower. Remembers towels, pajamas, thongs, soap, washcloths, toothbrushes, toothpaste, bath toys. Marches clean children out of the shower. Finishes his shower with cool to cold water.
(We know one father in charge of Shower Duty who counted swim time in the lake as a cleansing experience.)

_____ Potty Patroller
Knows the ins and outs of every rest stop along the Interstate. Carries toilet seat liners in back pocket, toilet paper in front pocket.

_____ Table Tackler
Scans menu in two seconds, deciding on everyone's culinary needs. Cuts food, catches food, picks up: food, pacifier, cup, fork, spoon, books, and cleans hands and faces while finishing leftovers.

_____ Private Eye
Constantly in motion—grabbing little hands trying to slip away. Eyes never really see sights but are glued to familiar backs of little people darting through crowds.

_____ Shlepper
Carries backpack, frontpack, hip pack, totes, food, jackets, sunglasses. Pushes stroller or carries child in child carrier. For unknown reasons, is often the family's Private Eye.

HOW SHOULD WE HANDLE MISBEHAVIOR?

When our children misbehave on a trip, we often don't know how to respond. At home, the child may just need time out —quiet play in his room, far away from us. Sometimes we need time out—quiet time by ourselves.

So what happens when Matthew screams in a restaurant or Toby throws a tantrum in the museum? Everyone seems to be staring at us. We're tired and so is he. Our first impulse is to scream back, or duck under the table, or drive home—without the screamer.

Mom and Dad's Handy Guide to Handling Misbehavior

1. Beware of your first impulse.
2. Watch your tone of voice. Be firm but friendly.
3. Remove him: Take a walk to the bathroom, car, or around the block.
4. Be sensitive to fatigue. Remember you're all sleep deprived.
5. Be consistent. If you say you're going to do something, do it.
6. Follow through on consequences. "The bear is mine today, because you hit your brother with it."
7. Offer alternatives. "Would you like to take a nap or lie quietly on your bed?"
8. Give your child a chance to behave positively. "Who wants to help me find a restaurant in this guidebook?"
9. Show a united front as much as possible.

Parents' Pet Peeve Quiz

Do you answer in unison or have widely different expectations about your kids' trip behavior?

Bedtime should be:
_____ rigidly enforced at _____ o'clock
_____ convenient to parent's schedule
_____ late so kids will sleep in late
_____ other:

Mealtime should be:
_____ quiet: no kicking, hitting or sliding under the table
_____ time for Mom and Dad to talk, uninterrupted
_____ family discussion time with Mom and Dad each sitting next to a child
_____ other:

Public behavior should be:
_____ not taken too seriously; everyone has bad moments
_____ consistently cooperative without whining or crying
_____ without sibling fighting
_____ other:

Misbehavior should be:
_____ handled just like at home
_____ dealt with leniently; he's probably tired
_____ a time to remove him from the group
_____ other:

MEALS

If you've ever had a tantrum in front of your children because your husband insisted on breakfast at a fast food restaurant and you were in the mood for flowers, waiters, fresh fruit, hot coffee, homemade danish . . . the works . . . you know why meals are a flammable issue.

Open communication is essential between every member of your family. Is Mom expecting several fancy meals at well-known gourmet restaurants? Is Dad hoping to try the local ethnic food? Do the kids expect lots of snacks and a hamburger at every meal?

You've Got to Eat, But How, When and Where?

Have each family member decide what he expects the meals on the trip to be:

_____ leisurely   _____ regional
_____ fast   _____ gourmet
_____ moderate   _____ fast food
_____ fancy   _____ ethnic
_____ nutritious   _____ other:
_____ all of the above!   _____ none of the above!

Parents plan to:

_____ eat at our usual meal times
_____ eat at convenient times
_____ allow more snacks, pop and sweets
_____ stick to house rules on snacks, pop and sweets
_____ choose restaurants according to my plan
_____ give each child a chance to pick his favorite type of food

ACTIVITIES

Design your trip before you leave. Try to combine fast paced, structured days with relaxed, unstructured days.

Decide:

• How much time will be devoted to:

_____ children's activities

_____ shopping

_____ adult activities

_____ fooling around

• Is one parent attending a conference or convention? How much time will the other parent and children be on their own?

• Will you encourage daily:

_____ quiet time

_____ nap time

_____ early bedtime

• Check sites that require tickets in advance

Parents remember to be:

• flexible . . . . the unexpected will probably occur.

• organized . . . . ten minutes before departure you certainly will not find the timer for the house lights. You probably loaned it to a neighbor.

• sensitive . . . . each family member has needs; it's best to take them into account (especially your own).

• humorous . . . . if you leave your sense of humor at home, your packing is incomplete.

• rested . . . . a family vacation is exciting, fun, adventurous and memory filled. Notice we didn't say restful. Begin your trip well rested and your relaxed attitude may be contagious!

THE FAMILY MEETING

Talk about vacation plans and make group decisions. This can best be accomplished through a FAMILY MEETING.

Philosophy: From pre-schooler to parent, everyone has a busy schedule. Designate a time to talk, to make decisions, to establish family unity. No one is left out and important family decisions aren't made five minutes before darting off to work. Children cooperate more fully when they've helped in the planning.

Ground Rules:
1. Select a meeting time that's convenient for everyone.
2. Prepare an agenda, but invite additions.
3. Allow everyone the opportunity to talk.
4. Don't ask for opinions on an issue that is nonnegotiable.
5. Rather then majority rule, aim for a consensus. (Two adults can railroad ideas through, but real cooperation won't follow if kids feel coerced.)
6. Have someone act as secretary to record the proceedings.
7. Some families rotate the chairmanship for each meeting.
8. Don't turn this into a gripe session, or a gang-up on one person.

Logistics:
1. Meet two or three times before the trip.
2. Limit the meeting time to hold everyone's attention.
3. Include all family members.

How to Reach Consensus:
1. Ask for what you want.
2. Be specific, "I'd like to sleep in twice during the trip, while you watch the kids." Rather than "I want some rest."
3. Be friendly; an agreement is a commitment between two or more people, not a demand.
4. Invite all family members to ask for what they want.
5. Don't sulk if you can't have it all!
6. Ask the children also. (If they get two fast food meals and one romp through the park, they'll be more understanding during your trip to the Art Museum.)

Suggested Topics:
1. What will make the car trip easier for you?
2. How can we help Dad (Mom) have a relaxing vacation?
3. What activities would you like to do on our vacation?
4. What should be the duration of our trip?
5. How should we handle misbehavior in the car?
6. What can we do to make bedtime go smoothly?
7. What healthy snacks would you like for the car ride?
8. Do we want to eat breakfast at a restaurant or in the room?
9. What would you like to do on our first day?
10. What types of new food would you like to try on our trip?

KEEPSAKE PAGE: "WHAT I EXPECT FROM OUR TRIP"
(Include each family member's quotable quote)

Every morning on this trip I'd like to . . . .

The best part about this trip is going to be . . . .

When I'm on vacation I really like to . . . .

I hope . . . .

An ideal day on my trip would be . . . .

33

KEEPSAKE COLORING PAGE

Offer children crayons or markers and ask them to draw a picture of themselves on vacation doing something they expect to do.

NOTE: A child may draw in the space provided or draw on separate sheets of paper (especially if there are siblings). Staple or tape the drawings to this page.

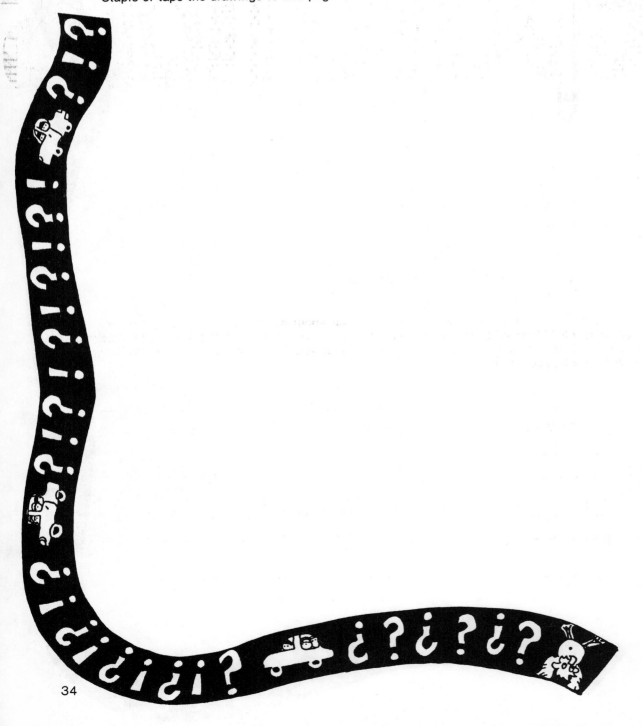

Preparations

WHAT TO CANCEL, WHOM TO NOTIFY, WHAT NEEDS CARE!
(How to Put Your Life on Hold)

A friend recently complained that after telling everyone on her list about her family's vacation plans, she felt a newspaper ad or billboard would have reached just as many people with less time and effort. We don't advise you to announce your vacation plans indiscriminately, but for the safety of your home and out of courtesy to friends, neighbors and delivery people, you'll need to:

_____ Newspapers   from _____ to _____   _____

_____ Mail   from _____ to _____   _____

Deliveries:	Phone #:	Services:	Phone #:
_____ milk _____			
_____ vegetables/ _____ fruit			
_____ laundry _____		_____ insect spraying _____	
_____ UPS _____		_____ water condition- ing _____	
_____ water _____		_____ cleaning _____	
_____ Other:		_____ garbage pick up _____	
_____		_____ Other:	
_____		_____	
_____		_____	

35

Notify

Phone #: _____

_____ family: _____

_____

_____

_____ building _____
         superintendent

_____ employer _____

_____ business _____
         associate

_____ answering _____
         service

_____ regular _____
         babysitter

_____ day care _____
         center

_____ school office _____
         (so absence can be
         accounted for)

_____ school teachers _____
         (to get homework and
         let teacher know
         reason for absence)

Phone #: _____

_____ neighbors _____

_____

_____

_____ police _____
         department

_____ office _____

_____ volunteer _____
         co-worker

_____ household _____
         help

_____ children's extra-curri-
         cular lessons:

_____ piano _____

_____ art _____

_____ sports _____

_____ tutor _____

_____ others: _____

_____

_____ extra-curricular clubs:

_____

_____

_____

HINTS: We urge you to continue your grass cutting or snow removal if you'll be gone for a while, so your house looks
         lived in.

Some families do not stop certain deliveries or services. They have reciprocal agreements with their neighbors to care
for each other's home.

Dear Jean,
Thanks for watching the house while we're gone!

Please...
Bring in the mail. Grab the newspapers too. (on Sunday we get 3 papers, don't forget the one in the screen door).

Accept UPS deliveries on Mon. Wed. & Fri.

Feed the fish, remember to only put about 5 flakes in every morning. between 10 & 12.

Cut the grass on Wed. Be certain to water the lawn if it doesn't rain by Thursday. Water the vegetable garden twice a day, especially the tomatoes. Feed the cat at 4pm daily. Rub her back and remember to say, "nice Kitty... Kitty", so she doesn't claw up the furniture. Bye till the 4th!

We must be honest. We've accomodated neighbors who've left us lists like this, but we were not very happy while they were gone. Unless you have a very fair reciprocal arrangement with a neighbor, or your neighbor happens to be your mother, we urge you to think twice before asking for so much help.

HINTS: • Check your calendar. Be sure you've notified or cancelled all social engagements, club meetings, extra-curricular activities and volunteer responsibilities that will take place while you'll be gone.

• Look ahead to your first week back. Is the Cub Scout Meeting scheduled for your house the day after you return? Is a special report for the office due the week after your trip? Are all your bills due the day you come home?

• Before you leave, re-schedule, or take care of any important time-consuming responsibilities or events that will take place soon after your return. Why ruin the last few days of your trip worried about what awaits you on return?

_____ water plants
_____ water lawn
_____ shovel walk, driveway
_____ other: _____
_____

_____ water garden
_____ cut lawn
_____ feed, walk pets
_____ other: _____
_____

WHAT DO I DO WITH SPOT?

If SPOT is a fish . . . . check out a time-release fish food now on the market.

If SPOT is a cat . . . . ask a neighbor to feed him and hope he doesn't take revenge.

If SPOT is an iguana, gerbil, hamster, or guinea pig . . . . maybe your child's class or camp would like to keep him for a while?

If SPOT is a dog . . . . leave him with: grandma   friend
                                           babysitter   nearby
                                           neighbor   farm or
                                                          kennel

He may return home dirty, or sick or with fleas, but taking him along may be a lot worse!

DISGUISING THE HOUSE
(How to look like you never left)

Even if you stop your mail, paper and services, and leave SPOT in a kennel, there are still many ways to have your house look lived in.

_____ place the lights on timers, several around the house, going on and off at staggered, but believable times.
_____ outdoor/porch lights on photo-electric cell timers
_____ radio or television on timers
_____ telephone bell tone turned to lowest volume
_____ one car left in the garage
_____ footprints, and car tracks around the house in snowy weather
_____ snow removal
_____ lawn and bushes trimmed
_____ garden and flowers watered

HINTS: Many community police stations have a Vacation Homewatch System. You may sign up and the police will check your home each day to make sure it is secure.

PACKING

Traveling by car presents a temptation often hard to resist. We tend to overpack, filling up every available space in trunk, backseat or car-top carrier with items we just can't do without.

The night before a trip we run around the house, yelling at our children while searching for clothes and vital possessions. We stay up past midnight trying to stuff things into an already bulging suitcase. By morning's departure we are cranky and upset.

Often our children will refuse to wear what we have planned or their pants will be too short or too tight. In all of the ruckus, we will forget to pack our bathingsuits and the pants to our husband's sportcoat will be left hanging in the closet.

Whether you are an impulsive last-minute trip taker or a well-organized list maker, we invite you to follow our packing guidelines. We have found they make the difference between a cluttered, frustrating trip and one where almost everything is anticipated.

for Packing

STEP #1: Determine your trip's purpose and activities:

Several weeks before you pack, start thinking about the clothes you'll be taking for your children in terms of your trip's purpose and the activities each family member will participate in. Of course seasonal considerations and temperatures count. We suggest watching the national weather listings in your local newspaper for two weeks prior to your trip.

THE FOLLOWING CHECKLISTS SHOULD HELP YOU DETERMINE YOUR TRIP'S PURPOSE AND ACTIVITIES:

PURPOSE

_____ Family/Friends visit   _____ Visit a theme park   _____ Camp in a tent
_____ Family reunion   _____ Tour a large city   or cabin
_____ Family/Friends affair   _____ Attend a conference/   _____ Relax at a resort
_____ (Other)   convention   _____ Visit a small town
                                   _____ (Other)   _____ (Other)

ACTIVITIES

_____ Fancy restaurants   _____ Museums
_____ Family dinners   _____ Plays or shows
_____ Parties   _____ Sporting events
_____ Fast food and family restaurants   _____ Zoo
_____ Picnics   _____ Aquarium
_____ Kitchenette meals   _____ Hiking
_____ Parks   _____ Walking
_____ Beaches   _____ Summer sports
_____ Worship Services   _____ Winter sports
_____ Swimming   _____ Others:
_____ Others:
                                            _____
_____

STEP #2: Determine Clothing Needs:

The purpose and activities of your trip will determine your children's clothing needs. Here is a list of the many clothing categories to include in your planning:

_____ **Dress clothes:** Worn for religious services, adult parties, and fancy restaurants. Be sensitive to an individual child's desire to dress up.

_____ **Casual clothes:** worn just about anywhere. Includes mix and match outfits, jogging suits, comfortable jeans, T-shirts and slacks. For the girls, sweatshirt dresses and casual skirts.

_____ **Cozy clothes:** Worn to travel in, or to curl up after a long day. These are the children's favorite, most comfortable clothing, often well-worn.

_____ **Active wear:** Worn to participate in outdoor or indoor sports or activities. Consider the specific sport and possibility of participating. Swim suits, jeans and leggings are in this category.

_____ **Outerwear:** Each child should have two outerwear garments. One may mysteriously get misplaced or dirty!

• Summer: Light sweaters, jackets and sweatshirts with hoods are highly recommended.

• Rain: Plastic fold-up rain coats in a pouch are inexpensive and easy to carry in totes and purses. Waterproof summer jackets with hoods are another good alternative. Don't forget umbrellas.

HINT: If you expect rain, take along an extra pair of shoes and socks for each child.

• Winter: If your trip includes outdoor winter sports, take two jackets for each child or check to see if there is a clothes dryer on the premises.

HINT: When traveling by car in the winter, all passengers should have snow gear—boots, hats, snowpants, gloves—just in case of an emergency.

_____ **Underwear:**

HINT: For one week or less, take two pair of underpants per child per day for 5's and under. If you are going for more than one week, plan on doing laundry.

_____ **Pajamas:** We have found that two pair per child for three's and older are usually enough. The number of PJ's for under three's must be decided on an individual basis. Count the number of PJ's your child uses for a week.

_____ **Infants:** Many parents plan at least four sleepers per day.

HINT: T-shirts and jogging pants can always double for PJ's. Robes are very bulky. Leave them home unless you will be staying with family and friends and your children are old enough to be modest.

_____ **Foot gear:** Don't forget sneakers for everyone—or some form of sturdy walking shoe. Even a trip to a zoo can turn into a family hike! No matter the purpose, or activities planned, each child needs at least two pair of shoes in the event of unexpected mud-puddle stepping or blisters!

Leave slippers at home and take thongs, which are terrific for beach, pool and showers.

Socks, tights and legwarmers round out the list of foot gear. Although one family, whose trip consisted of miles of city walking, insists that bandaids belong in the foot gear department.

_____ **Head gear:** Hats are necessary for both summer, as a sun protector, and winter, for warmth. Take extra hats if you will not be close to stores. Remember: In winter if your head is warm, your body stays warm.

HINT: Three's and older will appreciate sunglasses on sunny days. Dads and Moms need sunglasses for day-time driving.

Clothing for Moms and Dads

- Pack extra clothes. Children seem to get adults dirty. Just imagine being in close proximity to a drippy ice cream cone. Think about sitting on a park bench previously occupied by someone else's candy bar-munching kids.
- Denims wear well and are versatile. Moms can use a denim skirt or dress, to be "dressed up" yet still be appropriate for playground or park.
- Gym shoes are highly recommended for a day centered around children's activities such as parks, playgrounds, theme parks and beaches. If you're caught in a rainstorm, your shoes will dry.
- Comfortable walking shoes are a must for all outfits, even dresses. You'll never know when your day will involve walking.
- Be aware that delicate fabrics may get ruined. That silk blouse may never be the same after your seven-year-old gives you a greasy-handed hug in a restaurant.
- If you're comfortable, you'll be less cranky when the going gets rough. If you're not concerned about your clothes, you'll be more at ease.
- Don't forget one or two outfits you may wear for dress up.

STEP: #3: Putting It Together

- Take only clothes your children like to wear.
- Take washable clothes.
- Resist taking expensive specialty outfits that could be ruined and do not match other clothing.
- Before packing, always try on new clothes and off-season clothes.
- Try to wash all new clothes before packing to be sure they don't shrink or run.
- Layer It. It's easy to put on layers of T-shirts, shirts, sweaters, sweatshirts and jackets, or socks, tights, and legwarmers. Peel them off one by one should it warm up.
- Color Coordinate. You'll get better mileage out of your children's individual tops and bottoms if you take along one or two color families: blues and reds, beiges and browns, purples and pinks.
  Children will be able to coordinate their clothes with ease and they'll look "put together" with minimal effort.
- Use Disposables. Whenever possible, take toiletries, diapers and baby bottles that can be discarded when used. Their space will make room for things children like to collect on trips: rocks, shells, ticket stubs, post cards and souvenirs.

STEP #4: Determine Your Values

You need to explore your feelings about how others view your children. Is it important to you that your children look clean, color-coordinated, well put together with shirt tucked in and belt on? For that matter, is this important to your children? We know many nine-year-old girls who are very concerned with fashion and match even their barrettes to their outfits.

Another issue to explore is whether you dress your children differently on a trip to see friends and family than on a trip where you are "incognito."

There are no correct answers. We have heard from over two hundred parents and still found no consensus of opinion. It is important that each family discusses these issues and agrees on basic clothing values.

We'd like to share one mother's personal anecdote. We hope it puts into perspective the information given so far about planning your children's clothing.

"When we go to a family camp one week each summer, I pack my children's oldest, most spotted and ragged clothing. I want them to feel relaxed whether they build sand castles, paint, picnic or hike.

When we tag along as part of my husband's yearly professional conference, I dress the children like mini-adults. We usually stay in luxury hotels and take the children with us to all the adult functions: parties, fine restaurants and nightclubs. The boys take mostly mix and match knit shirts, slacks and sweaters. The girls take dresses and skirts with blouses to interchange and pant outfits for colder climates. The children actually enjoy looking 'adult' and act accordingly."

STEP #5: Involve Your Children

The temptation is to plan and pack when your children are busy or sleeping. However, we've found great benefits in including our children in planning and packing. Of course the amount they participate must be appropriate to their ages and to your comfort level.

We urge you to begin even at an early age with simple planning. Have several items out and let your child pick which one he wants to take.

Even if you must plan out the clothing entirely by yourself, at least give your children a few choices. Let them make the final decision among the clothes you have deemed appropriate.

The benefits of allowing children to participate in planning and packing will be evident throughout the trip.

1. They might become self sufficient and take pride in how they look.
2. They know what goes with what and where it is.
3. They look forward to a trip by choosing clothes for specific days or events.
4. Power struggles with tired children decrease. When he wants the red shirt that is still at home you may gently remind him that he decided to take the blue one.
5. You'll take only clothes your children like and enjoy wearing.

Another way to involve your children during packing is to have them pack their Busy Kit.

Children love deciding which toys, books, art supplies, cards and games to take. They will involve you in grand discussions about which stuffed animals should be packed. They will spend days changing their mind and repacking their kit.

HINTS: • Remove the kit a day or so before you leave to be sure it has anything left in it.

• Set limits. The over-stuffed, pot-bellied bear stays home, the tiny dog goes.

• If you have lots of extra room in your car, you might consider taking extra toys your child wants to bring. One unsuspecting father packed into the trunk all the boxes he thought held the trip's necessities. Reaching their destination, he found one box filled only with dolls and doll clothes! His daughter enjoyed herself to the fullest on that trip.

• Be sure to ask your children if there is anything they'd like to bring or think you forgot to pack. More often than not, an observant eight-year-old will remember certain items that were indispensable on your last trip: that old picnic blanket, certain favorite beach toys, his warmest sweater, or his sister's favorite game. One six-year-old suggested taking the family's bath mat to place in the hotel tub so the kids could continue their nightly baths without slipping!

• We are not suggesting packing so many items that the parent who unpacks needs an hour's nap to recover. Also, don't make the offer of "what else would you like to take" unless you truly mean it!

STEP #6: Make a List or Use a Chart

We've given you the general clothing categories and suggested ways to decide what types of clothes to bring.

Now comes the hard part, actually choosing the clothes and making sure you've included enough of each category for each traveler.

One mother offered a great tip for packing her infant's clothes. "I put the suitcase next to his dresser and go through each drawer, pulling any clothes I think he'll need. Usually I find items I forgot about or haven't been able to find."

If you have two or more children, older than infancy, most likely their clothes will not all be found in their dressers. We have found clothing under the bed, stuffed between dresser drawers and in the back of closets. Stray socks have even shown up in the car.

In other words, you will not be able to go from dresser to suitcase. You will need to remember what clothes your child owns (he can often help you), find them, and be sure they're clean!

For this reason we recommend using a checklist or chart.

Checklist formats vary

A. You may be comfortable listing each family member and then itemize his needs by category:

Adam		**Samara**	
_____ pants	3	_____ slacks	2
_____ belt	1	_____ barrettes	
_____ underpants	5	_____ underpants	5
_____ T-shirts	3	_____ dresses	2

B. You may want to list only the items you may forget:

_____ belts   _____ pony tail holders

_____ tennis shoes

C. You may want to list needs by day:

Day 1 - DisneyWorld
Adam - shorts, shirt
       underpants, socks
       tennis shoes

Day 2 - Shopping
Adam - jeans, T-shirt
       underpants, socks
       shoes, jacket,
       clean outfit for dinner

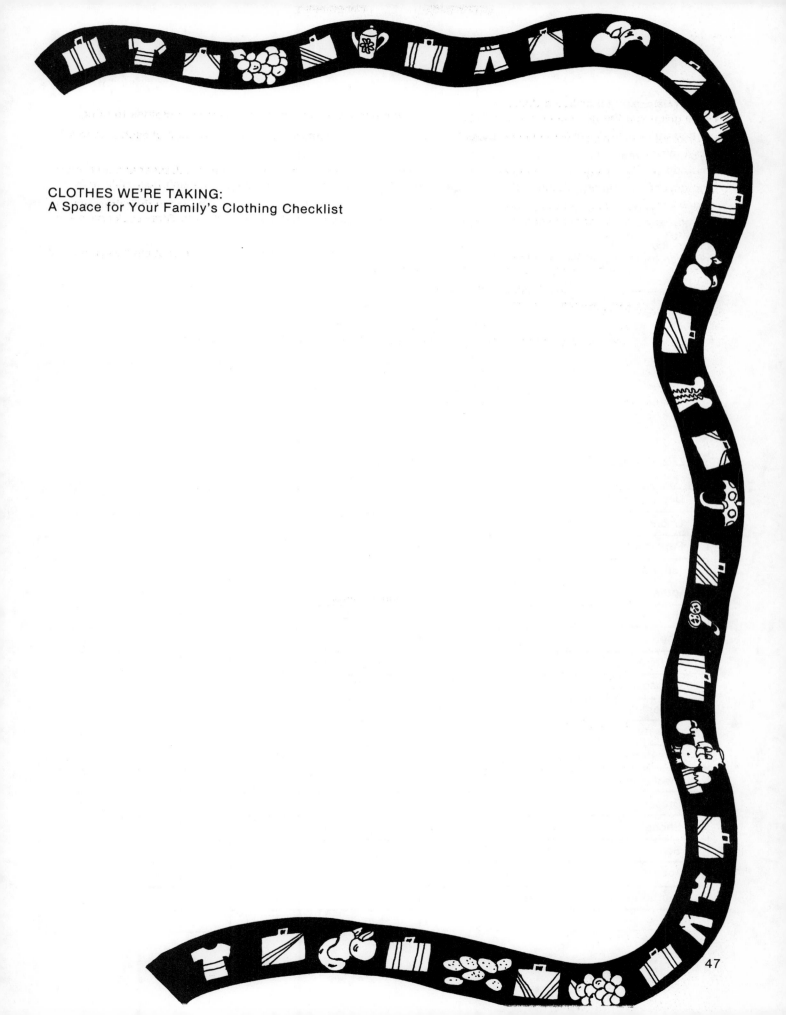

CLOTHES WE'RE TAKING:
A Space for Your Family's Clothing Checklist

CLOTHES WE'RE TAKING—A PACKING CHART

Organizational buffs might find making a chart suits them better.

A chart is a reusable form that can be filled in for any trip. One very organized mother of four described her packing method.

"A week before the trip I take out clothes and pile them on the floor of my bedroom. That way I know they'll be clean when I begin packing.

"I pile them as outfits: belts, barrettes, shirt and pants together.

"I check off the items on a mimeographed chart. I use copies of the same chart for all of our vacations and packing the children for overnight camp."

_____ Family Packing Chart

Trip to _____ for _____ days, on _____
DATE

	Name of each family member							
Number of each item being taken								
Underpants								
Undershirts								
Pajamas								
(other:)								
(other:)								
Slacks								
Shorts								
Shirts, t-shirts								
Dresses, skirts								
(other:)								
Jackets								
Sweaters, sweatshirts								
Swim suits								
Dressy clothes								
Shoes								
Socks								
Accessories (belt, barrettes, etc.)								
Toothbrush & personal toiletries								

STICKY SITUATIONS

Dress Clothes - How To Fake It.

Boys under five do not need a sportcoat and tie even if you are staying at a hotel that serves High Tea and has dinner seatings. We found that a navy sweater looks just fine with casual shirt and pants.

We recommend deck shoes as an alternative to buying expensive leather shoes for over fives who want to look dressy.

Girls often want to dress up when Mom does, so be certain to include some skirts or dresses. In the summer, sandals may double for party shoes; sundresses with a blouse underneath become jumpers.

The Almost Potty-Trained Child.

We recommend holding off toilet training until after a trip. Your child will be under less stress and will be happier performing his duties in a familiar environment.

Routines such as bed time and meal time are usually disrupted and not as predictable as at home. It is unfair to require your child to adhere to a toileting routine.

Grandma and Grandpa won't mind diapers when the alternative is a wet couch or carpet.

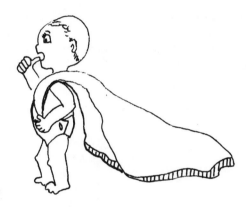

The Newly Potty-Trained Child.

We recommend patience or a back-up package of diapers offered in a kind, friendly manner. Children often forget about toileting when they are excited or tired.

Take extra pants and heavy training underpants and realize that you might have to do a load of laundry.

Use rubber pants over underpants at night or consider using diapers. Take note: Rubber pants over underpants may cause skin irritation in some children.

Believe it or not, potty chairs come in handy at rest stops, beaches and picnics. If your child is uneasy using the regular facilities, try to find a spot in the trunk for his potty chair.

Potty rings are much smaller and easier to carry, for those brave children who'll use the regular facilities, but still fear falling in!

Several mothers suggested carrying a package of toilet seat liners to use at each rest stop.

Nocturnal Swimmers (Bed Wetters).

We recommend bringing a plastic crib sheet or a plastic mattress cover or plastic utility bags to place over the mattress and below the sheets to insure your infant or older child a dry mattress each night. Remember to cut the utility bag open and to lay it flat on the mattress. Keep it away from small children!

Depending on your child's age, we recommend rubber pants at night over several heavy underpants. Again, be cautious of skin irritation.

Take several pair of pajamas and plan on doing laundry. Several parents of bed wetters reported rinsing out the wet clothing each morning in the sink and hanging it to dry.

Remember to bring a mild detergent.

One mom told us that her five-year old rinsed his own pajamas each morning in a spirit of cooperation.

Laundry: Should I Or Shouldn't I?

Whether or not to do laundry is a tough decision. Explore your priorities.

1. Are you willing to sacrifice time doing laundry in a laundromat when you could be visiting a new site?

2. Are you willing to do "household chores" on your trip?

3. Is there room in the trunk or car for extra underwear, PJ's and clothes that would keep you from doing laundry mid-week?

4. Are there convenient laundromats near your accomodations? One parent surveyed told us that on most family trips she swings through Cleveland to visit her folks and also do the laundry!

RULES TO REMEMBER

1. In general, kids do not stay clean.

2. Don't wear Grandma's special outfit in the car. Save it until you arrive.

3. Try everything on, especially if wearing off-season clothing. Kids grow faster than you think.

4. Check if clothes are clean before packing. Kids do put clothes away dirty.

5. Don't start planning the night before.

6. If they won't wear it at home, they won't wear it on vacation.

7. If you forgot it, you can buy it there.

8. If you can rent it, don't carry it.

9. Resist the temptation to buy all new clothes.

10. Don't travel in your best clothes! Kids have a tendency to get Moms and Dads dirty, too!

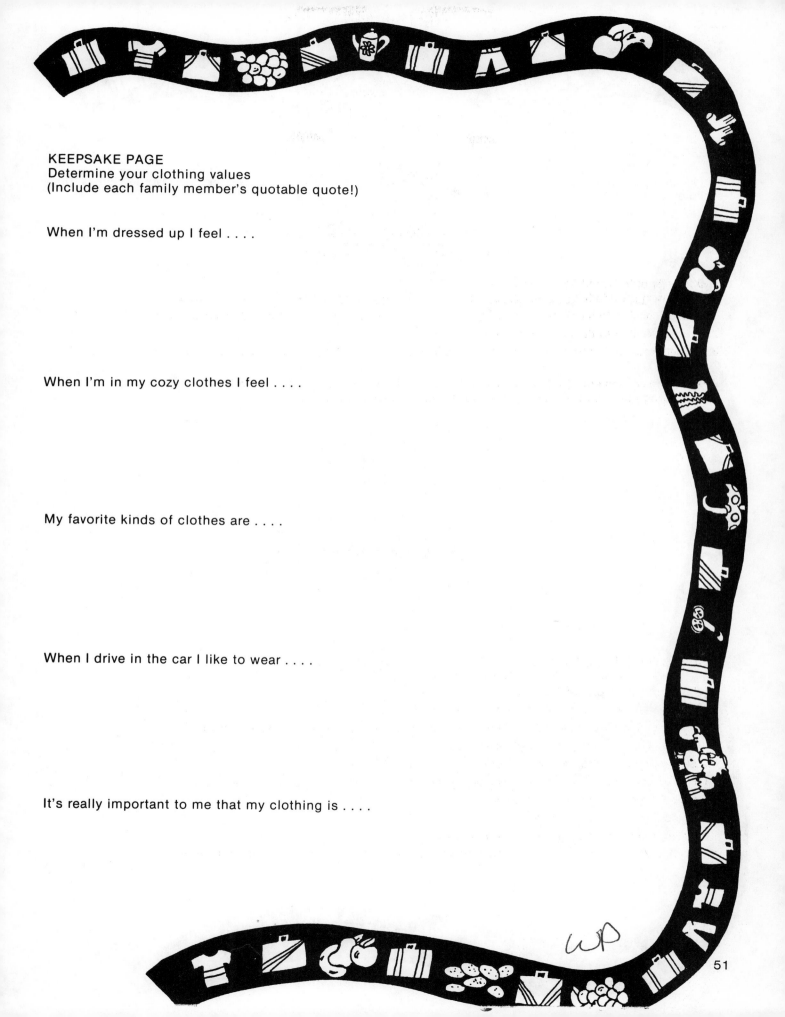

KEEPSAKE PAGE
Determine your clothing values
(Include each family member's quotable quote!)

When I'm dressed up I feel . . . .

When I'm in my cozy clothes I feel . . . .

My favorite kinds of clothes are . . . .

When I drive in the car I like to wear . . . .

It's really important to me that my clothing is . . . .

KEEPSAKE COLORING PAGE

Offer children crayons or markers and invite them to draw a picture of themselves in their favorite clothes. Urge children to include details like socks, shoes, hat, etc.

Note: A child may draw in the space provided or draw on separate sheets of paper (especially if there are siblings). Staple or tape the drawings on this page.

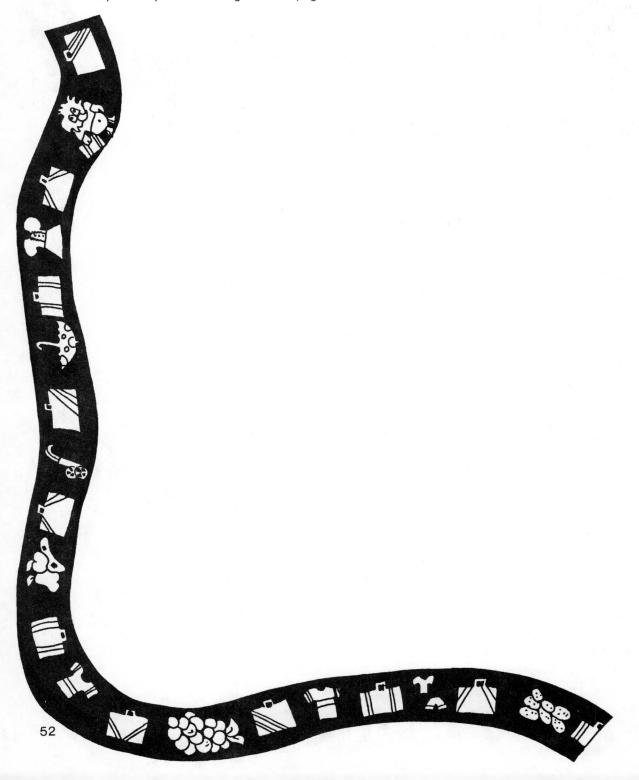

Methods

of Packing

IN WHAT SHOULD I PACK ALL THIS STUFF?

There are four distinctly different carriers to use when you pack. We found a combination of carriers is often the best approach.

SUITCASES

Advantages:
- sturdy
- clothes easily seen when open
- stacks easily in trunk
- clothing remains safe and unwrinkled

Disadvantages:
- limited space
- requires folding and some organization
- odd size gear, bedding and toys won't fit
- you wouldn't want to repack dirty, sticky or sandy clothing

HINTS: • Small containers placed inside your carriers will keep your items organized.
- Many moms suggested packing their clothes in "lingerie holders." Approximately 26" x 16", they have four or five clear zippered pockets that hold socks, underwear, pajamas and small items. They roll up and may be placed in the corner of a carrier.
- Toiletries will stay together in plastic toiletry bags, cases or rolled holders.
- Plastic sandwich bags will hold barrettes and odds and ends.

DUFFLE BAGS

Advantages:
- fits in more clothes than conventional suitcase.

- can be used as convenient dirty laundry bag.

- holds sporting equipment, games, stuffed animals, rain gear, shoes, boots, bedding and diapers.

- clothes require little folding.

- could be used as a pillow or divider in back seat of car.

Disadvantages:
- can't see what's inside.

- clothes become wrinkled.

- odd size might not fit into your trunk.
- other flat items will not stack well on top.

PLASTIC LAUNDRY BASKETS
Advantages:
- clothes require little folding.

- doubles as dirty laundry basket.

- sand falls through mesh.

- clothes are very visible

- holds odd-size sporting gear, diapers, shoes and toys.

LARGE PLASTIC BAGS
Advantages:
- inexpensive duffle bag.
- doubles as dirty laundry bag.
- small enough to fit into trunk's odd spaces.

- holds diapers, bedding, shoes and toys.

Disadvantages:
- rips easily.
- empty bags unsafe around small children.
- only appropriate for casual trips (camping, cabin, motel).

- can't see what's inside.

Disadvantages:
- requires a lot of space (van or large station wagon).

- only appropriate for casual trips (camping, cabin, motel).

- items could fall out and become lost.

HOW SHOULD I ORGANIZE ALL THIS STUFF?

There are three popular ways to organize your family's clothing when you pack. Which you are comfortable with would depend on your children's ages and your personality.

Divide by Family Members
Each person in your family has his own bag, duffle, basket, small suitcase or portion of a suitcase.

Advantages:
- Everyone is responsible for his own clothing.
- Everyone knows where his clothing is packed and can get to it easily.
- Each child carries his own bag.
- Fights over possessions would decrease.
- Unpacking on the trip and setting up each person's space would be quicker.
- No one could be blamed for another's wrinkled or missing clothes.
- Each person could leave his clothes inside his own carrier and not unpack during the trip.

Disadvantages:
- You might not have enough carriers for each person.
- You could end up with more pieces of luggage than you want to carry or can fit into your trunk.
- Small children may decide during the trip that they are too tired to carry their own bag.

HINT: Some parents enjoy packing clothes for each child as daily sets of shirt, pants, belt, socks and underwear. This helps the child become responsible for getting totally dressed.

Divide by Clothing Categories
Divide your family's clothing into categories. The entire family's pants and shirts would be in one case, underwear and pajamas in another. Similar items are packed together.

Advantages:
- If small children require your help to get dressed, packing their clothing with yours would save time and minimize the number of bags needed.
- If your family arrives at a destination and jumps right into activities before unpacking, you could locate appropriate clothes quickly.

HINT: Many families go for a swim on arrival, and need to find bathing suits promptly. Others tuck in their children for nap or bedtime on arrival, and want pajamas or "lovies" handy.

Disadvantages:
- Your children will constantly need to go through your clothes to find theirs.
- Your older children will still want to unpack their clothes and keep them separated from everyone else's.
- Figuring out whose-is-whose will be difficult if your children are close in age or size.

Divide by Family Groups
Clothing is packed according to logical family groups. Parents may pack together in one case, while children pack in another. The clothing for male family members is packed in one case, with clothing for female family members in another. Any grouping that may prove helpful during the trip is encouraged. If big sister and little brother share a suitcase they may help each other during "getting dressed" time.

Advantages:
• This method combines the best of the two previous methods.
• Your children are responsible for their own clothing.
• Everyone can find his clothing easily.
• Your clothing packed apart from your children's will stay intact.
• Grouping the children's clothing together could foster cooperation between children.

Disadvantages:
• If your children are fussy about their clothing or possessions, they may balk at sharing cases.
• Conflicts and frustrations might increase.
• If your children are close in age or size, their clothing will look alike and cause confusion (especially underwear!)
HINT: One mom, with several daughters close in age, packs separate plastic bags with each girl's barrettes and underpants and labels the bags by name.

Some meticulous packers have even suggested the following method:

Divide by Days
Although this method sounds horribly complicated, it has its advantage. It is best used when:
• You drop off Child A on Day 4 with Grandma and continue your trip with Children B, C and D.

Pack Child A's clothing for Day 1-3 with the rest of the family. Child A's clothing for Day 4-on should be packed separately.

• Your trip is separated into distinct parts and clothing needs. For example, Day 1-3 is at the seashore or beach. Day 4-5 is at a Family Affair. Day 6-7 is at a theme park. It would be convenient to pack clothing according to each separate part of your trip.

HOW CAN I FIT IN ALL THIS STUFF?

Some people intuitively know how to fill every space. They leave nothing dangling over a suitcase edge, never omit important items for lack of room. Their key to success, they say, is in the technique.

Rolling
Most clothes can be rolled and pressed against surface edges of suitcases or into empty spots in duffle or other pliable carriers. This is especially true for T-shirts, underwear, socks, pajamas, and most baby and under-two clothing.

Layering
Rather than placing into suitcases piles of neatly-stacked folded clothing, stagger and overlap the piles. Less gaping space will be left.

Filling
Be on the lookout for inner spaces you can fill. Shoes offer a perfect space for rolled socks. Purses may hold barrettes, makeup, belts and other small items.
HINTS: A tightly-packed suitcase will keep clothing in place and cause fewer wrinkles.

Some people place the largest items into the carrier first. Smaller items will fill in remaining spaces. Others put their suits and dresses on the top and have fewer wrinkles.

RULES TO REMEMBER

1. Some families label all carriers with tape to indicate:
   - general contents (so you don't have to keep peeking)
     whose clothing?
     what categories?
   - specific number of clothing items for younger children (so you'll keep track of what's still clean)
2. Let your family's compulsive packer pack the different carriers and car trunk. He usually gets more in!
3. Be sure your name and address tags are on the inside and outside of your carriers.
4. Let your children have their own personal suitcase or bag—if not for their clothing, then for their BUSY KIT. For young children, this will be one of the trip's highlights and they will probably carry their bags everywhere.
5. Many families enjoy having each family member pack individually, but still pack in a shared case certain items the family is sure to use together.

We suggest category or group packing with the following:
- Toiletries—in makeup bag, small suitcase, or toiletries bag
- Beachwear—swim suits, towels and toys in large mesh plastic tote
- Sleepwear—in section of a carrier or in a separate bag

ACTIVITIES FOR KIDS DURING PACKING TIME

1. Invite the child to inventory his clothes. The older set may create a list, while the younger set may pretend they work in a store, counting their stock.

   Parent needs to supply: paper and pencils. If children can't write have them draw the object.

For example:

   5 pants

   3 dresses

   Additional Fun: When parent comes in to pack, the child must subtract the number of items put into the suitcase.

2. Encourage the child to take his favorite dolls or stuffed animals on an imaginary trip. Ask him to get them ready and plan where they are going.

3. Offer paper and crayons with these instructions: Imagine the World's Largest Suitcase, now draw a picture of what's in it.

   Additional Fun: Save these drawings to discuss on the road!

4. Offer your child the opportunity to help by folding, stacking, organizing and counting as you pack.

5. Hire a babysitter or mother's helper to keep children occupied while you organize.

HINT: Although we are strong advocates of participation by children, we urge every parent to set realistic goals. Young children may not have the patience to proceed in an organized manner. Older children may want to bring every article of clothing they own. Set limits and a structure that you're comfortable with.

6. Urge your child to pack his own toys, games etc., to create his Busy Kit. Jointly decide on the container used. For example: a canvas bag, or back pack.

KEEPSAKE PAGE:

"Our feelings about packing for a trip"
(Include each family member's quotable quote)

While we were packing I felt . . . .

If we left anything out I will . . . .

Now that we're packed I am . . . .

KEEPSAKE COLORING PAGE:

Offer children crayons or markers and invite them to draw a picture of the family packing for a trip. Urge children to include all family members doing something.

NOTE: A child may draw in the space provided—or draw on separate sheets of paper (especially if there are siblings). Staple or tape the drawings to this page.

Kits

Create your own kits for the car, restaurant, daily excursion, or emergency situation. Well-conceived kits have eased lengthy car trips, and made eating in restaurants a pleasure.

WHAT IS A KIT AND HOW DO YOU CREATE ONE?
By our definition, a kit is a complete and portable package of something fun or fundamental.

KITS MUST BE PACKED IN APPROPRIATE CASES:

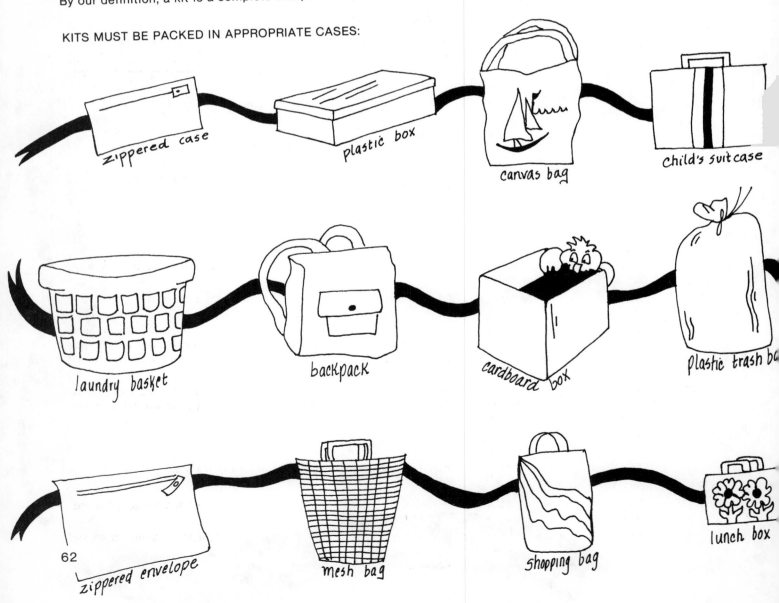

zippered case

plastic box

canvas bag

child's suitcase

laundry basket

backpack

cardboard box

plastic trash bag

zippered envelope

mesh bag

shopping bag

lunch box

KITS MUST BE PLACED IN CONVENIENT SPOTS

Mom's purse, the car glove compartment or trunk, at arm's length in the car.

HINTS: Keep the kit for its specified activity. The fastest way to make a Restaurant Kit unappealing is to let your child use it for two hours in the car!

Certain kits, like the First Aid Kit, should be packed away in a closet or cupboard to remain intact for the next trip. Before each trip, be sure to check your kit to add anything missing.

Certain kits should never be put away. They should remain in your trunk, purse or near the back door. Some of our best trips were last-minute day trips. Our kits made the difference between fun and frenzy. We suggest keeping on hand: Day Kit, Beach Kit, Restaurant Kit, Porta-Changing Table Kit and Car Kit.

Don't take too much! One mom reported that the back seat of the car looked like a four-family garage sale after only two hours on the road!

BUSY KIT

USES: To pass the time in the car, or hotel, in solitary play.

CASES: Plastic box, zippered case, lunch box, school bag or canvas bag, preferably with shoulder strap.

CONTENTS: Paper, crayons, markers (if you don't mind colorful children), stickers—preferably from the office supply store (sheets of dots or squares are available in many colors). Plasticene (a molding clay that does not dry out) with a few plastic dinosaurs for imaginary play. Any small plastic toys are appropriate. Activity, coloring and reading books. For the older child: scotch tape, paper clips, stapler, and manilla folders for organizing and collecting his souvenirs.

PHILOSOPHY: This offers children structured fun and promotes quiet activity while driving or waiting in a hotel. Children should always pack this kit, and be responsible for keeping the contents intact.

An added
attraction: Some parents gather small toys from around the house, some frequently used, others mildly ignored, and wrap them in wrapping paper. These packages are offered throughout the trip with the statement, "Look what wanted to come along . . ." Other parents purchase small inexpensive items and offer these wrapped packages at intervals.

RESTAURANT KIT

USES: To pass the time constructively and take the children's mind off of hunger while waiting for a meal, or while other family members finish their meal.

CASES: Small cases, like a pencil case for older children, a canvas bag for a younger child.

CONTENTS: For young children: a bib, wipes, crackers, and a few small toys. These toys should be special—perhaps purchased solely for this kit, or used infrequently at home. (Suction toys are great for highchair trays and car windows.) For older children: crackers, crayons, paper, mini notebooks, colored pencils and activity books. These supplies should be new, and reserved only for restaurant time.

PHILOSOPHY: Even the hungriest child will respond to crackers and enjoy drawing with you until the waitress arrives with the food. Keeping the contents only for meal time often encourages children to play quietly, while parents have time to relax.

MOM AND DAD'S EARLY MORNING COPING KIT

USES: To occupy early risers and give Mom and Dad their dose of early morning coffee.

CASES: Small box, plastic bag, shopping bag.

CONTENTS: Small electric coffee pot or hot pot, coffee, cream and sugar, mugs or styrofoam hot cups, spoons, and packages of hot cocoa mix for the children.

    HINT: Hot pot can double as a baby bottle and baby food warmer. Be careful not to scald your hand from the steam when removing the bottle or jar!

PHILOSOPHY: This offers a bright beginning to the day!

DAY TRIP KIT

USES: To carry necessities for a day's outing, making a return trip to the hotel unnecessary.

CASES: Totes and backpacks.

A NOTE ON BACKPACKS:

These come in many sizes and are appropriate even for children to carry. Several families report that a child's good intention to carry the backpack often dissolves as the day wears on. A child's backpack should be adjustable so an adult can carry it. Other families have the adults wear backpacks.

CONTENTS: Include whatever you may need for one day:

_____ snacks

_____ drinks (water may be carried in a plastic cup with a lid)

_____ straws, paper cups (these come in quite handy for splitting large drinks or for a quick drink from fountain or sink)

_____ wipes, washcloth

_____ mini-First Aid Kit: "band-aids," tissues, suntan lotion, aspirin or aspirin substitutes, needle, thread, safety pins, small scissors

_____ change of clothing for each child (several extra shirts for 2's and younger)

_____ some adults even report including an extra shirt for themselves!

_____ jackets or sweaters for everyone

_____ rain gear if rain is even a remote possibility

_____ extra shoes and socks are nice for a possible downpour

_____ barrettes and rubberbands for long hair

HINT: Several mothers reported including their purse contents within their backpack to lessen the number of items they carried.

CAUTION: This is a comprehensive list that will be too heavy for most backpacks. Carry only essentials on your back. Extra items can stay in your trunk.

PHILOSOPHY: The success of a day's outing hinges on proper preparations. Clothes or supplies left at the hotel are of no use when a lap is splashed with milk or a heel develops a blister.

CAR SAFETY KIT

USES: To provide for any unexpected emergency such as car trouble, inclement weather or minor accidents.

CASES: Boxes, bags, totes

TRUNK CONTENTS: Spare tire and necessary equipment
Tool box
First Aid Kit

Winter necessities:
* Clothes: gloves, mittens, hats, boots, scarves, and extra clothing layers for EVERYBODY, even adults. Bring several blankets, too!
* High energy snacks:
  unsalted nuts (for appropriate ages)
  raisins
  dried fruit
  crackers and peanut butter
  boxes of juice (even if they freeze, you can peel off the box and eat the frozen juice bar like a popsicle)

- Emergency:
    salt—for melting ice, old rug,
    collapsible shovel, ice and snow
    scrapers, old gloves for handling
    salt, flares, transistor radio,
    flashlights and batteries

Summer necessities:
Several light-colored towels or blankets to place over hot, dark-colored seats, hot seat belt metal or baby's car seat.

HINT: Many families feel their "CB" (Citizens Band Radio) is reassuring for long car trips.

GLOVE COMPARTMENT

CONTENTS: Flashlight, maps, paper, pencils, tire gauge, folded paper towels, paper toilet seat covers, tissues, old rags, your road service card.

PHILOSOPHY: We encourage all families to think carefully about car safety and to anticipate all unexpected problems.

HINTS: Don't bury your Car Safety Kit under your luggage. Be sure you have easy access to it.
Please have your car checked before a trip. Most automobile safety experts recommend checking the following:
1. tire pressure and tread
2. level of oil, anti-freeze, coolant, battery and power-steering fluids
3. lights and turn signals
4. windshield wipers
5. all hoses and connections for leaks
6. GAS TANK! (Never go below ¼ full in winter!)

CAR SANITY KIT

USES: To promote a congenial and cooperative trip by providing all sorts of activities and diversions.

CASES: Bags, totes, boxes, lunch box

CONTENTS:
- Food and Drink
- Quiet Toys: magnetic puzzles, stickers, word search and activity books
- Travel Games: miniature store-bought games, imagination games, word games
- Comfort Items: pillows, special "lovies," blankets, "necessary bottle" (or plastic urinal with lid) for small children's toileting relief, one roll of toilet paper
- Necessary Equipment: lap trays, clip boards

PHILOSOPHY: With enough variety of things to do, we hope families will have many long stretches of undisturbed car travel, punctuated by only occasional outbursts of, "He kicked me," He has his leg on me," and "When do we get there?"

BABY'S PORTA-CHANGING KIT

USES: To be prepared for baby's frequent changes, feedings and entertainment with everything organized in one spot.

CASES: Diaper bag, tote, backpack, bag

CONTENTS: For changing:
- blankets
- flannel-covered rubber "puddle pads"
- lots of disposable diapers
- cloth diapers (for wiping and drying)
- creams, powders
- masking tape to close diapers whose tags are no longer sticky
- rubber pants
- diaper pins
- wipes, wet washcloth in a plastic bag
- extra sleepers, clothes, socks or booties
- plastic bags for soiled clothes

For feedings:
- bibs
- bottles
- snacks
- drinks

- spoon, cup
- teething ring
- pacifier

For entertaining:
- "lovies"
- rattles
- books

- favorite squeeze toys
- stuffed animals

PHILOSOPHY: Many parents reported they were reluctant to bring their infants along on family trips with older children. We find infants are wonderful travelers and are usually easy to please when all of their needs are anticipated and organized into one bag.

FIRST AID KIT

USES: To be prepared for minor accidents, illness, bruises or cuts. Most families reported they needed a first aid item at least once every trip.

CASES: Although commercially prepared kits are available, we recommend making your own. You will be able to personalize the contents with your medicine brands and family needs.

Use shoe boxes, plastic boxes, large toiletry cases.

CONTENTS:
_____ dosage chart for your children's ages for each medicine you include
_____ your pediatrician's phone number
_____ any current medicine a family member is taking
_____ aspirin or aspirin substitute
_____ antihistamine for allergic reactions and insect bites
_____ throat lozenges
_____ cough medicine
_____ decongestant
_____ antiseptic
_____ sun screen
_____ Calamine lotion
_____ Vaseline
_____ insect repellant
_____ "diaper rash" cream
_____ sunburn ointment
_____ motion sickness pills
_____ thermometer (rectal for baby)
_____ tweezers
_____ sharp needle to remove splinters (sterilize first)
_____ ear plugs
_____ tissue
_____ for poison aid: Syrup of Ipecac
_____ for insect sting aid: Prescription from your doctor

_____ powder
_____ hand cream
_____ flexible plastic strip bandages such as "band-aids"
_____ absorbent cotton
_____ cotton-tipped swabs
_____ sterile gauze bandages, assorted sizes ½"-2"
_____ sterile gauze pads, assorted sizes
_____ nail file and nail scissors or clipper
_____ small utility scissors
_____ needle and thread
_____ safety pins
_____ measuring spoon and cup
_____ first aid tape

PHILOSOPHY: Even though each of these items could be purchased when and if needed, we've found that the moment of need is precisely when we are back at our accomodations and the stores are closed. Better to bring everything and be prepared.

DIRTY CLOTHES KIT

USES: To wash out soiled clothes needed to continue trip, such as: bedwetter's PJ's, underwear or clothing with accidental spills.

CASES: Plastic bag, tote, section of a larger case

CONTENTS: small plastic bottle of liquid detergent
small travel envelopes of soap powder
spot remover
clothes pins
collapsible hangers
plastic bags (to bring home damp clothing)

PHILOSOPHY: Anticipate accidental mess, wet PJ's or a short supply of underwear. Washing clothes out in the sink is efficient and easy. BRINGING A DIRTY CLOTHES KIT ENCOURAGES THE FAMILY NOT TO OVER-PACK!

HINT: Even if you don't plan on doing laundry mid-trip, you'll still need a container for storing dirty clothes. A duffle bag, pillow case, large plastic bag or plastic laundry basket works well.

Equipment

When traveling with children under three, the following equipment is highly recommended to free up hands, ease muscle strain and bring along the comforts of home.

_____ **Cloth Front Baby Carrier (for infants).**

Baby nestles next to your heart and usually sleeps while you maneuver around. This is a very satisfying experience for both parent and child. We've seen many dads enjoy this togetherness with their infant.

HINT: Baby and parent may get rather overheated, so in warm weather, be certain the carrier is light-weight cotton, and the adult is lightly dressed.

_____ **Backpack Child Carrier.**

Carry your child and offer him sights and experiences he'd miss if he were "down-under" in a stroller. Also, the backpack frees up your hands. Great for walking over uneven terrain where a stroller would be inconvenient, or in crowds.

HINT: Try out the backpack before the trip. Your child may need to get used to this method of travel. You may need to get used to the weight on your shoulders.

_____ **Collapsible Stroller.**

Excellent for long leisurely strolls in cities, big or small. You can easily go on and off bus or subway by collapsing the stroller and carrying your baby.

HINTS: Bring along all detachable parts if you have room. Sun roofs and carrying totes come in handy.

Certain brands of collapsible umbrella-style strollers can be joined together side by side if one adult is responsible for two small children.

_____ **Child's Harness.**

Ideal for the parent traveling along with an active toddler, or for a large family.

HINT: Using a child's harness is very controversial. If you use one, your child should be comfortable, both physically and psychologically. Many parents feel a harness is "no way to treat a child." Others feel a harness allows their child freedom of movement without worrying he will roam away.

_____ **Backpacks (Pack this with your suitcase to use when needed).**

Carry your Day Kit items, purse contents and rain gear on your back as an alternative to shoulder or arm totes. Your arms and hands will be free to hold your children's hands. Backs carrying packages seem to hold out longer than arms.

HINT: Practice carrying a backpack before your trip. If older children want backpacks too, invite them for a practice walk around the block with a full pack. If they are still interested in taking their backpack—great! You'll have to carry less. Many mothers complain about purses that become painfully heavy, loaded down with necessary trip paraphernalia. One mother told us how she returned from vacation with a severe and reoccuring pain in her right shoulder. She later realized it was from her heavy shoulder bag!

There are other pack options available at most sporting goods stores:

_____ **Fanny Pack.**

Carry your lunch, a sweater, baby's bottle, a diaper, and odds and ends in this pack that hangs from a belt around your waist.

_____ **Hip Pack.**

Carry your wallet and odds and ends in a pouch the size of a pocket that fits onto your belt.

_____ **Roof-Top Carrier.**

Maximize the space available within the car in order to minimize your children's fights. Even parents with station wagons told us, "We put as much on top of the wagon as possible to provide more space inside to play games or stretch out. The more cramped, the more tense."

HINT: Make sure you have the proper supports on your car roof for a heavy carrier. Be sure the lock works.

_____ **Luggage Rack.**

Offers a similar option as the roof-top carrier but is vulnerable to theft and inclement weather.

_____ **Clip Boards.**

Give children a flat, hard surface on which to color and draw.

_____ **Lap Trays.**

Children have a spot on which to eat, play games and draw. More all-purpose than clip boards and will store under the front seat.

_____ **Car Seats**

A must for children under two years old and under 40 pounds.

Even if your child can legally sit without a carseat, many parents find their children enjoy riding in a cushioned seat that puts them high enough for an unobstructed view out the window.

Children also seem to be less car sick when sitting supported and higher up.

_____ **Sassy Seats.**

An alternative to a high chair, these collapsible seats hook onto tables. Many parents would rather carry this than wait for the one or two highchairs available at each restaurant.

_____ **Potty Seats and Potty Rings.**

_____ **Porta-Cribs.**

This collapsible crib is perfect for the young baby, if you'll be staying with friends or family.

HINT: Although hotels have cribs, we recommend calling to ask about the vintage of the equipment. What is safe for a two-year-old might not be appropriate for a six-month-old.

Many babies fall asleep easier when surrounded by familiar objects. We recommend bringing baby's bumper pads, crib sheets and a few of his favorite crib animals.

_____ **Suitcases on Wheels.**

Nothing is more gratifying than watching your four-year-old pull one of the suitcases through the lobby or parking lot while you carry Baby, two Busy Kits, a Porta-Changing Table Kit and another suitcase.

_____ **Coolers.**

Keep your food, drinks, baby bottles cool and fresh.

Use freezer pack like "blue ice." Lasts approximately one day depending on your cooler.

HINT: Make your own freezer pack by filling a plastic milk carton with water and freeze it. Then as it defrosts, you have cold water.

Use ice cubes in plastic bags. Be sure the bags are securely closed.

_____ **Thermos.**

Terrific for bringing cold or hot drinks depending on the season. Children love having their own thermos full of a drink (we suggest water) included in their lunch box.

_____ **Plastic Cups with Tight-fitting Lids.**

Instead of, or in addition to a thermos. Offers a lightweight option for carrying drinks.

TRAVEL FOODS

WHEN DO WE EAT?

Food and travel go together. Ask any five-year-old what he wants to do during the long drive and he'll probably mention one or two of the snacks he saw Mom getting ready for the trip.

Certainly, food is brought along on car trips not just to stave off hunger while we look for suitable picnic grounds or restaurants. Some of us use food as a diversionary tactic, when Jennifer is kicking Barry. Some of us use food as a bribe, so Jason will sit up straight, or as a way to ease our children's boredom; "When will we be there, Dad?"

As parents concerned about our children's health and caloric intake, we urge you to examine your values about food. Are your children allowed snacks at specified times? Does it matter if everyone is hungry when you stop for a meal?

We feel strongly that sensible eating in moderation, is a habit we should exercise all the time, in all places. Many of us use trips as an excuse to overeat and indulge, then regret it later. Children stuffed with chocolate won't relax easily or drift quickly off to sleep. A parent, who just went off his diet, may feel grouchy.

WHAT SHOULD WE BRING?

The following snacks adhere to our rule that foods eaten in the car should avoid being excessively:
1. salty
2. messy
3. crumbly
4. meltable

Great snacks for the car or picnic:
_____ cheese cubes
_____ hard-boiled eggs
_____ cold chicken
_____ sandwiches cut in squares
(jelly, peanut butter, cheese,
cream cheese)
_____ unsalted crackers
_____ bagels
_____ unsalted nuts (for appropriate
ages)

_____ plain cookies such as
vanilla wafers or ani-
mal crackers
_____ granola bars
_____ rice cakes
_____ snack-pack cereals
_____ fruit rolls and fruit
bars
_____ raisins
_____ trail mix (nuts,

_____ unseasoned popcorn (for appropriate ages)
_____ bananas
_____ seedless grapes
_____ fruit (sliced and peeled for young children)
_____ dried fruit
_____ raisins, dried fruit)
_____ cucumber slices
_____ carrot sticks
_____ celery sticks
_____ other favorites

HINTS: Fruit sliced into pieces will not turn brown if dipped in lemon or orange juice.

Carrot and celery sticks can be prepared ahead of time and kept fresh in a container of cold water. Drain off water before packing.

In the summer, stay away from foods that spoil easily like mayonnaise or spreads.

Many parents like to pack one or two Suprise Snacks. You know best what would excite your children and still be within your definition of an acceptable treat.

Some parents save certain snacks for the following day's drive.

CAUTION: PREVENT CHOKING

Offer food that is appropriate to your child's age. Choking is a serious possibility when foods are round and moderately hard. If your child is a "stuff as much food as will fit in the mouth" eater, choose your car snack cautiously. For those under three, we suggest LEAVING OUT popcorn, nuts, carrots and hard candy.

Drinks for the gang:
Many parents take only ICE WATER as a drink. Ice water does not stain or become sticky when spilled and it really quenches thirst.

Some parents like bringing frozen cans or frozen boxes of juice. The juice defrosts as they drive and remains cool.

One mom suggested taking frozen grapes to suck on in the summer. (For appropriate ages only.)

Children love drinking out of their own spout-top thermos or spout-top plastic cup. Pack the thermos or cup in lunch boxes so children may help themselves.

CAUTION: Limit beverage intake somewhat, unless you plan on stopping every half-hour!

FOODS FOR BABY

_____ cheese cubes
_____ bananas
_____ unsalted crackers
_____ Cheerios or Chex cereals
_____ dried toast

_____ teething cookies or
       bagels
_____ formula - powder, cans,
       or disposable bottles
_____ juice
_____ sterile water in jug

A Note on Baby Food:

Take the smallest size jar of store-bought baby food. This way you will not be tempted to save what is left. Use extreme caution in re-using open baby food. Frozen home-made baby food defrosts in the car by meal time and would be convenient for meals on the first day of your trip.

A Note on Formula:

Take a jug of sterile water to prevent problems for baby. Water varies greatly from region to region and babies' stomachs are sensitive to this.

Never save leftover formula.

Clean bottles and nipples thoroughly to prevent bacterial growth.

Many mothers like to take bottles they have pre-filled with powdered formula. Then they add water when needed.

If your baby no longer uses formula, always buy fresh milk. Be sure the container is sealed and the label states it is pasteurized.

A Note on Nursing:

Even if you have established a fine nursing routine, we recommend taking along bottles for water, juice, or formula supplement. While we've had many positive experiences nursing during our trips, in gas stations, restaurants, museums and amusement parks, be prepared for the unexpected or emergency situation that could be created if:

• You become ill and must be put on medication.
• The weather is very warm or baby is ill and needs additional fluids.
• A family member or friend offers to babysit and you are able to leave the children for a short time.

NON-FOOD ESSENTIALS

_____ napkins
_____ paper towels
_____ plastic bags and ties
_____ disposable moistened towelettes
      (If your children are past wearing diapers, take individually wrapped towelettes. A large container is bulky and
      tends to dry out before you have a chance to use it all.)
_____ plastic silverware (or at least one knife, fork and spoon)
_____ plastic spoons and bowls (if you'll be eating cereal in the hotel room)
_____ can opener
_____ straws
_____ plastic tablecloth or blanket for picnics
_____ paper plates
_____ hot/cold cups

For Meals In Accomodations: (Kitchenettes, Cabins, Condos)
Call first to see what your kitchen is supplied with. One family found everything necessary including a corkscrew, while another family found empty cabinets.

Add the following:
_____ aluminum foil
_____ disposable aluminum pans
_____ sponge
_____ liquid detergent
_____ sharp knife
_____ large spoon
_____ hot pot
_____ mugs
_____ small pot with lid

HINT: Kids love shopping for food at local stores. We do too; it makes us feel like natives!

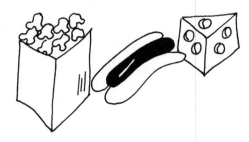

HOW SHOULD WE CARRY IT?

Many families put their snacks in a large bag or cooler kept within reach of a parent. Inside are individually-wrapped snacks, large packages of snacks, and paper goods.

Many parents like to control snack disbursement. Others like to have the children take turns deciding what's next and passing it out.

In addition to the cooler or large bag, some families encourage each child to pack a lunch box full of individual snacks and a drink. Our children love this sense of responsibility and independence. Having their own snack box, with a few toys included, heightens their sense of adventure.

Lunch boxes also make ideal tables from which a child can eat his snack or meal with little mess.

HINTS: • Coolers are essential if you will be driving several days or planning to feed your children one or more meals in the car or in your hotel room. Many parents told us they saved time, money and stress by serving breakfast in their hotel room.

• Never place the cooler in the trunk. Place it as low in the car as possible (hot air rises) and out of the sun's rays.

• Store your cooler in the bathtub of your hotel room—if you spring a leak as the ice melts, you won't cause a flood.

KEEPSAKE PAGE

Here's a spot to list everyone's favorite munchies. To many people a car trip means lots of snacks. (Include each family member's quotable quote!)

When I go on a long car trip I like to munch on:

KEEPSAKE COLORING PAGE:

Pretend the world has turned into yummy food. Draw a picture where every object is something to eat. (Ideas: The tree bark is chocolate, the grass is green beans, etc.)

NOTE: A child may draw in the space provided or draw on separate sheets of paper (especially if there are siblings). Staple or tape the drawings on this page.

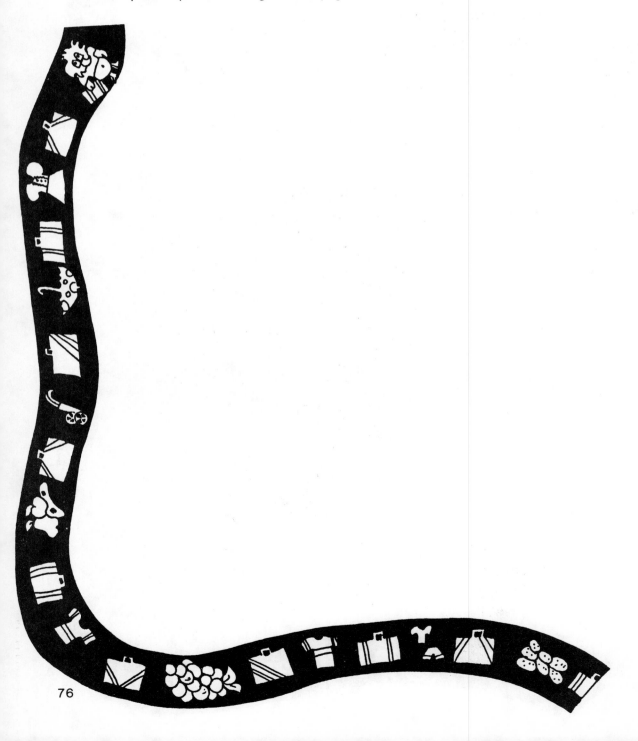

TWO MINUTES BEFORE BLAST OFF

You're exhausted, but you made it. Suitcases are packed, food is ready, kits line the backseat. Spot is at the kennel, the kids are wearing their sunglasses and clamoring to leave. It's that time . . . . BLAST OFF is only a few minutes away. So what if you're already two hours off schedule?

Time to check just once more.

Did you remember to bring:
_____ prescription sunglasses
_____ all suitcases or carriers
_____ an alarm clock and nightlight
_____ jackets for everyone
_____ your camera
_____ your wallets (with money, traveler's checks and/or credit cards)
_____ emergency phone list (neighbors, pediatrician)
_____ Health Insurance I.D. numbers, card or forms
_____ car insurance and car registration
_____ stamps and addresses for postcards
_____ plastic bags
_____ food and drink
_____ diapers
_____ first aid kit

Did you remember to:
_____ call the answering service
_____ close all house windows
_____ turn down heat and air conditioning
_____ lock all doors and secure the house
_____ stop your mail, paper and deliveries
_____ diaper the baby one more time
         and
_____ TAKE ALL THE KIDS!

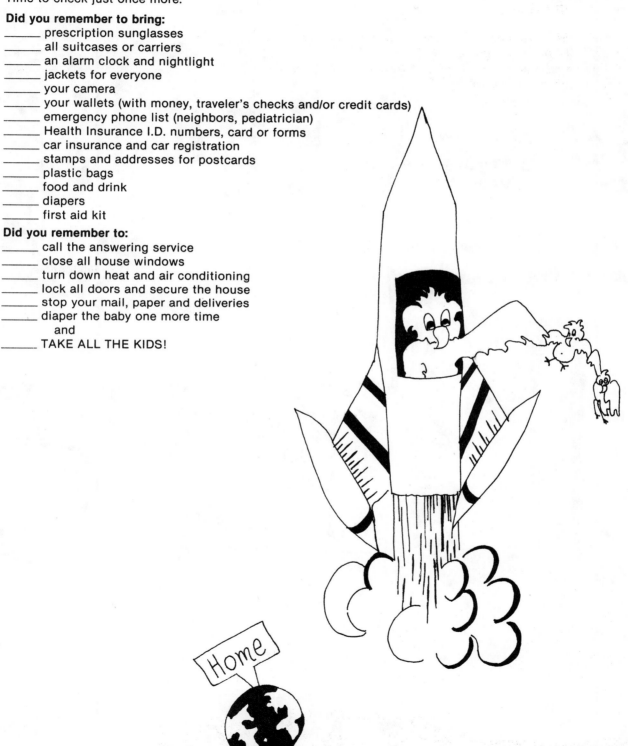

Getting There

SANITY

Many of us believe the family trip begins once we reach our destination. The car ride, whether one hour or several days, is seen only as a means to get us there. We disregard the needs of our passengers, particularly our kids, and set unrealistic driving schedules.

We leave too early and drive like maniacs. We ignore the pleas of stir-crazy kids and a speed limit obeying spouse. Full bladders, empty stomachs, cramped legs and throbbing headaches must wait. The schedule must not be upset. We must make good time, or if we're really lucky, arrive ahead of schedule.

This sets us up for frustration, anger and disappointment. The kids fight and whine; we yell and threaten. Why didn't we just stay home?

The truth is your family trip begins as soon as you walk out of your house, close the door behind you and step into the car, settling down with maps, food, pillows and toys.

If you plan your drive as the first leg of your family trip, you will have more fun. Remember, it's supposed to be an adventure. Take your time, drive a reasonable amount each day, stop often and plan to take in a few sights along the way.

WHEN SHOULD WE LEAVE?

Some families like leaving early morning, while it's still dark. These hardy souls pack the car the night before, scoop up their sleeping children and take off into the semi-darkness. After driving two to three hours, they stop for breakfast.

Some families time their departure after dinner and drive all night. This schedule certainly avoids the whining and restless child syndrome, since young children sleep most of the way. However, driving at night poses hazards to anyone not used to it.

CAUTION: The next morning the kids will be well rested and energetic. You'll be ready for a nap.

Some families leave mid-morning after a hearty breakfast. A full night's rest and a full stomach begin the trip on a relaxed note.

Some families leave early in the morning before breakfast. They pack a sack breakfast for each family member. The kids are busy eating for the first half hour or longer. (An added bonus—the kitchen is left spotless).

Some families with older children maximize daytime driving. Leaving early in the morning gives children plenty of daylight for activities.

HINTS: • Pack your car the night before departure. You'll feel less rushed the next day and will be less likely to forget something.

• Tell your kids what time you'll be leaving and how long the trip will take.

• If your spouse chronically leaves things for the last minute, accept this quirk. Plan your departure later or give him an earlier departure time to compensate for his habitual lateness.

• Don't rush everyone through breakfast. Indigestion is not a good travel companion.

• Let the kids run around and burn off energy before you leave.

HOW OFTEN SHOULD WE STOP?

Every family is different. We know a former long distance trucker who drives six hours between each stop. His children and wife have adjusted to this schedule. They leave at dusk and try to sleep most of the way. The day before departure, they begin to limit their fluid intake.

We know families with little driving tolerance who stop to stretch every 45 minutes. They can easily turn a four hour drive into a six hour adventure.

The key to success is discussing this before departure. Let the kids know how long they will need to sit still between stops. Be ready for spontaneous changes in your plan.

THE WIGGLE QUOTIENT QUIZ

What is your family's "Wiggle Quotient?" or How often will you need to stop?

Circle the responses that best describe your family. Then add the number of A's, B's, C's and D's. Your score will be interpreted at the end of the quiz.

1. Age of each child
   a) 9 to 12 years   b) 5 to 8 years   c) 1 year or under   d) 2 to 4 years

2. Number of children
   a) one   b) two   c) three   d) four or more

3. Number of children in the back seat
   a) one   b) two   c) three   d) four or more (you're tempting the fates unless you drive a van)

4. Parents' expectations
   a) This will be great.   b) I wish they were older.   c) How much longer?
   d) Why didn't we fly?

5. Number of hours parents slept last night
   a) 8 - 10 hours   b) 6 - 7 hours   c) 5 hours   d) not a wink

6. Parents' sense of humor
   a) And now for my Donald Duck voice...   b) Did you hear the one about...
   c) A flying hat is not my idea of a joke.   d) My head hurts too much to laugh.

   SCORE:

Mostly A's - Snap on that aviator helmet and drive on! We bet you can drive for at least six hours, and coast into a gas station when the gas gauge registers empty. Combine the gas station stop with a leisurely meal and an unhurried stretch.

Mostly B's - Fortify yourself with activities, food and charm. If the kids are isolated on either end of the back seat, occupied and full of goodies, you should be able to stop every two to three hours for potty patrol and kiddie runs.

Mostly C's - Take into account your kids' needs and you'll be in for a relatively smooth ride. If baby is awake, make lots of consistent (every two hours), short (10 - 15 minutes) stops. Keep switching food, drivers, seats and activities.

Mostly D's - Take a deep breath and pretend you're the Little Engine That Could. "I think I can; I think I can." Resign yourself to frequent stops. If you let your toddler run around every hour, he will cooperate better. Dangle carrots in front of the kids: "The fudge shop we stopped at last year is only 15 miles away. Sit quietly until our next stop and we'll all have a yummy treat."

WHAT ABOUT CARSICKNESS?

Although pediatricians assure us this isn't a common problem, too many of us have heard our kids whining, complaining they feel nauseous on a long car ride.

Long drives can bring on a queasy feeling even in the most veteran traveler, especially on winding or bumpy roads.

• **To help:**

Offer sips of cola (the sugar sweetened variety).

Offer sucking candy or lollipops (only to kids three years or older).

Offer snacks at intervals along the way.

Take time to stop, walk around and enjoy the fresh air.

Offer your shoulder and urge the child to take a nap.

Change seats.

• **To avoid:**

Don't offer reading material or coloring supplies to a carsick child.

Don't let the child overeat.

Consult your pediatrician before using an over the counter carsickness drug like Dramamine. One family used Dramamine for their daughter. She was cured of carsickness and slept the entire drive. The same family gave the same medicine to their son and he became grouchy and hyper-active.

When a child has had previous bouts of carsickness, he may be convinced it will happen again.

Be positive with him. Use the power of suggestion. Offer him his own can of cola with a straw and encourage him to sip often. Tell him this will do the trick.

Keep him busy with games that require talking or singing.

If all else fails, turn off to the side of the road, or have a large paper bag handy.

Try to anticipate the sickness. Don't make an already uncomfortable child feel worse by blaming him for the mess!

WHAT IF WE MUST COVER GREAT DISTANCES IN A SHORT AMOUNT OF TIME?

Drive when your kids are asleep.

Consider flying to your destination.

Recognize that a tight driving schedule will probably create a tense drive, complete with irritable kids and grouchy adults.

WHAT SHOULD WE DO WHEN WE STOP?

We wish we could put the car in gear, seal the doors and windows shut and drive automatic pilot all the way to our destination. But we can't. We have to stop sometime, if not just to stretch and change drivers, then certainly for potty patrol.

There are many reasons to stop between stretches of driving. When the Sardine Can Syndrome strikes, and everyone is ready to explode, try some creative stops. (Every stop should always include potty patrol. Adults included.)

• EXERCISE: Do aerobics, play follow the leader, or catch. Take at least ten minutes to walk around and stretch those legs. Breathe the fresh air.

HINT: Even babies need exercise. Let baby lie on your lap and kick, or gently move his legs up and down.

- SWITCH: Switch drivers. Put an adult in the back seat with the kids. Put one kid in the front seat.

- EAT: Buy food at a local store, then picnic. Try a local ice cream parlor. Do the fast food routine or dine at a "real" restaurant.

- PHOTOGRAPH: Take pictures of each other and the scenery. Don't forget to include the trusty car. Take turns snapping the shutter. The three-year-old will like this opportunity.

- VISIT: Turn off at a town to visit a historic site or natural wonder. Visit friends or family mid-way to your final destination.

- COMBINE ACTIVITIES: Try a few all purpose stops. Find a rest area with a gas station, picnic area and general store. Or drive off the freeway into town to find a restaurant and take a stroll. An hour stop may allow you to drive for a longer stretch.

- SEIZE THE MOMENT: We've coasted into small towns and found ourselves in the midst of a festival, county fair, sidewalk sale or marathon race. We've turned down the scenic highway and found breathtaking overlooks, a rock collector's dream and secluded picnic spots.

Unplanned and unexpected events can turn out to be the highlight of your trip. Relax. You'll get there. So what if you're several hours off schedule? (Just be certain your hotel is guaranteed for a later arrival).

- SCHEDULE ADVENTURE: Rather than fast food restaurants, have a picnic in a park, after a stop at a small neighborhood market. Ask the locals about the town, about special sights and local parks.

Rather than drive for long hours, break up the trip with a stay overnight. Be sure the hotel has a pool. Unwind in the water before bedtime. Wake up the next morning refreshed.

TIME SAVING TIPS

1. Eat in the car; run around when you stop.
2. If the kids have taken off their shoes and jackets, be sure they put them back on before the next stop.
3. Picnic instead of waiting in a restaurant.
4. Limit drinks.
5. Insist that everyone "try" at every stop.

How Do We Maintain Our Sanity?
We would be less then honest if we said our trips always go smoothly—no crying, no fighting, no tantrums, no disagreements.

These behaviors are often inevitable when five people are stuck together for hours at a time in a cramped space.

With practice, we've found ways of reacting to poor behavior and ways to encourage cooperative behavior.

DO'S AND DON'T'S FOR POSITIVE TRAVELING

DO:

1. **Have a positive attitude.**
   Keep repeating: "This is going to be fun!" or "I'm looking forward to a week with the kids!"

2. **Keep your sense of humor.**
   An unexpected tickle or joke often diffuses the tension.

3. **Understand the importance of space.**
   A handy guide: your car size is directly proportionate to the level of sibling fighting, noise and parental frustration.

4. **Keep your car organized and clean.**
   You might have to clean out the car at every stop and re-organize the kids' toys.
   HINT: Some parents stay organized by storing art supplies and small toys in old shoe organizers pinned to the back of the front seat.

5. **Anticipate problems.**
   Don't ignore your kids' needs, likes and schedules. Anticipate when they'll be hungry, need to use the bathroom and how long they can go without jumping around. Divert fighting caused by boredom or lack of exercise with a new activity.

6. **Rotate seats.**
   Play musical seats every few hours. Take turns sitting in the front and back. Changing seats will give everyone a new buddy and a fresh view.

7. **Switch drivers.**
   Give yourself a break. Drive for a while. Let your spouse take a turn as moderator, teacher, camp counselor and tour guide. Relinquish the treat bag and the crayons. Squint into the sun and watch the yellow line waver back and forth. It will be relaxing.

8. **Offer choices they can't refuse.**
   Do you want to take a five or 15 minute nap?
   Do you want to sit quietly in the front seat or the back seat?
   Do you want to stop for ice cream now or after dinner?
   Do you want to sing songs or play rhyme games?

9. **Fill in the blanks:** If you guys do _____, we'll be happy to do _____ for you. (For example: If you sit quietly for the next ten minutes, we'll stop at the nearest fast food restaurant for a drink.)

10. **Give undivided attention.**
    Sit next to the troublesome child (a favorite old teacher's trick). Read him his favorite story, play a game, let him lean on your shoulder and get snuggly.

11. **If nothing else works . . . .**
    Stop the car. Do something unexpected like calisthenics or have a hugging contest. Try running around to catch Dad and tickle him.

DON'T:
1. Don't expect the kids to misbehave, fight and be bored. They will.
2. Don't fan the flames or engage in a yelling contest.
3. Don't threaten or name call. You don't really want to leave Nicholas by the side of the road—do you?
4. Don't feel bad if strangers are watching your not-so-perfect kids.
5. Don't blame your kids for problems along the way.
6. Don't use punishment as your only means of control.

HINT: If you decide to take away a special dessert, treat or privilege as a punishment, remember . . . .

• It's difficult to be consistent on a trip.

• It's even more difficult to follow through if you'll be spending time with family or friends who have planned a full day of treats and special desserts.

• Be sure you say something you can follow through and won't regret.

• Try to have the consequences follow as quickly as possible after the behavior. Then you won't be side tracked, forget, or give in to "Please, I'll never do that again, I promise."

• It's easier to punish the whole family or all the kids, rather than singling out one kid, who just might continue to misbehave because he is feeling so dejected and left out.

• Give everyone a warning before handing out the punishments.

• Don't go overboard. We once said, "No desserts until we get home!" in a moment of utter despair and regretted it every day after that.

Which takes us to the next point . . . .

• Don't be afraid to back down and explain that you did over react and you feel it makes more sense to modify yesterday's decree.

A NOTE ON YELLING
If you must yell . . .

• Realize you are normal and just reacting to a lot of pressure.
• Don't get carried away.
• Stick to "I" statements that describe how you feel. "I am so angry!" "I am so upset!" "I am not able to handle this noise!"
• Try not to viciously attack your kids' personalities, manners, demeanor, or values. You'll feel better yelling if you don't wound the kids in the process.
• Remember, it feels better to let off steam, but in the cramped space of a car, all loud noises sound even louder.

WHEN THINGS GET OUT OF CONTROL AND OTHER STORIES OF THE OPEN ROAD (AN ASIDE FOR PARENTS WHOSE SENSE OF HUMOR NEEDS RECHARGING)

It happens only blocks from home, less than fifteen minutes into the family vacation. Personalities change. Kids and parents undergo a strange metamorphosis.

A precocious, adorable, cooperative kid becomes:

THE SNIVELER:
He cries, complains, moans, sighs, whines. "He hit me." "I'm hungry." "I'm tired." "I can't sleep." "I have no room." Nothing is suitable; everything is annoying and upsetting.

THE QUESTIONER:
He asks the same simple questions over and over and promptly forgets to listen for the answer. "Are we there yet?" "When will we get there?" "What time is it now?" "Are we stopping yet?" "Can we have our treat now?" "Are we there yet?"

THE SPRAWLER:
He invades the other kids' space, taking over the backseat with his legs, arms, stuffed animals, toys, crayons and magazines. The other kids sit on his toy dinosaurs and step on his discarded clothing.

THE ATTENTION SEEKER:
He has to use the bathroom as you pull out of the rest stop. He feels like throwing up. His feet fall asleep. His seat belt is strangling him.

THE THRILL SEEKER:

He dangles his toes tantalizingly close to your head while you try to nap. He waves frantically and makes faces at on-coming cars. He holds his sister's doll half in and half out of the open window. He picks up old chewing gum and bottle caps. He finds unwrapped candies in the crack of the seat.

THE PROVOKER:

He pinches his older sister and smiles contently when she shouts. He hides his younger sister's pacifier and listens angelically to her screams. He eats his brother's snack, then apologizes loudly to the unsuspecting sibling.

An understanding, responsible, loving parent becomes:

ROBOTON, THE SCHEDULED AVENGER:

He glues his foot to the gas petal, enters a trance-like state and erects an unpenetrable, sound proof partition between himself and the rest of the family. He will not relinquish the steering wheel; he controls the windows, radio and doors. Stops are based on his master schedule and his needs. "Pilot to crew. Come in. We will stop again in six hours. Over and out."

FRESSELLA, THE FOOD MAESTRO:

With sticky fingers, crumbs in his hair and wrappers obscuring his shoes, he keeps the bag of food at arm's reach. Orchestrating the trip into a food symphony, he doles out fruit, donuts, nuts, granola bars and cookies every mile, punctuates every conversation with a piece of gum and celebrates every new town with a candy bar. Good behavior wins a cupcake. "Stop fighting and you'll get a surprise."

MAPFISTO, THE HUMAN TRIP-TIK:

With maps, brochures, magazines, tour books and notepaper spread open on his lap, he holds a felt tip pen in mid-air, gesturing with it for emphasis. "Only 483 miles to go. Turn right at highway 108 for the six mile scenic drive. Stop after ½ mile for a great picture. In 15 miles, we'll be able to stop at that old country inn for breakfast. By my calculations, we'll be at the famous museum in time for lunch and if we get on highway 47 by 2:00, we'll drive 300 miles by evening and have dinner at one of the four gourmet restaurants written up in my magazine."

BACKSEATER, THE COMPLAINING AGGRAVATON:

He mutters and mumbles continuously under his breath. His hands flail wildly back and forth trying to swat backseat offenders, or clutch corners of moving clothing to offer quick non-verbal admonishments. He is in pain, in anguish, in agony most of the trip. "The car's a mess!" "You kids are giving me a terrible headache." "We're going too fast." "Not another stop!" "I knew my back would never last." "You're chewing your gum too loud." "I knew we'd get lost."

Safety

Car safety is serious business. Every family who has taken a car trip knows how important the kids' car behavior is to safe driving.

How well the kids behave in the car will greatly affect the driver's concentration and ability to follow safety rules.

We recommend teaching your kids car etiquette from the beginning, when they are still traveling in car seats, and consistently and emphatically enforcing your ground rules on every drive thereafter.

Whether it's a five minute drive to the grocery store or a two hour drive to visit family, kids need to know what is acceptable car behavior.

Parents and children must work together to have a successful and safe car trip. Please remember you are "hauling" precious cargo. Obey all traffic rules, don't take risks and only drive if you are in an alert and wakeful state of mind.

CAR ETIQUETTE
1. Seatbelts on whenever car is moving.
2. Voices low.
3. No flying objects.
4. Hands, feet and heads inside car.
5. No objects thrown out the window.
6. Never distract the driver.
7. Car doors always locked.

SAFETY TIPS

1. Anchor all objects. Keep the back window ledge clear. A sudden stop could send objects flying.
2. Never leave kids alone in the car. They may set the car in motion, become overheated or too cold, or attract strangers.
3. Never allow kids to leave the car without an adult. Kids are often too small to be seen over the side of the car.
4. Never let kids play with the steering wheel or controls.
5. Never cover the window with a dark cloth to shade kids from the sun. It could block the driver's view.
6. Keep on hand garbage bags for litter, and towels to cover hot car seats and seat belt buckles.
7. If a kid is sitting in the front seat, be certain he isn't distracting the driver, or kicking near the gear shift or gas pedal.

RED LIGHT RULE: IF KIDS NEED HELP, PULL OVER AND STOP THE CAR.

KIDS AND CARSEATS

Help your kids get used to carseats.

- Bring the carseat into the house.
- PLAY: Let dolls and stuffed animals go for a ride.
- PRETEND: Your kids can become astronauts, pilots and race car drivers.
- PERSONALIZE: Use decals, stickers, pictures. Make a special seat cover. Attach special toys.

Be sure the carseat is in the proper position and angle for your kid's size.

Place the infant seat diagonally in back of you, so you can see and reach baby better.

WHY CARSEATS?

- Carseats are comfortable, safe and secure.
- Carseats give kids great views out the window and cut down on car sickness.
- Carseats keep kids from becoming moving distractions.
- CARSEATS ARE NOW REQUIRED BY LAW IN MANY STATES FOR ALL KIDS FOUR YEARS AND YOUNGER. FINES ARE IMPOSED FOR NON-COMPLIANCE.

POTENTIAL PROBLEMS

- Be sure your carseat complies with the Federal Motor Vehicle Safety Standard and has been "dynamically tested."
- Be sure to follow the manufacturer's instructions for installing the seat.
- Be sure to line vinyl carseats with fitted covers or towels on warm days.

KIDS AND SEATBELTS

- Be a good role model.
- Be consistent. Everyone wears a seatbelt everywhere.
- Enforce your rules: SEATBELTS ON: WE GO. SEATBELTS OFF: WE STOP.
- Be sure the kids are comfortable.
- Be sure the kids are occupied with activities.
- Praise the kids for wearing their seatbelts.
- Place a smiley face on the sun visor when everyone is buckled up.

PLEASE DON'T COMPROMISE YOUR KIDS' SAFETY TO MAKE BETTER TIME OR HAVE FEWER ARGUMENTS. ALWAYS BUCKLE UP.

STICKY SITUATIONS

- Your six-year-old wants to nap. DON'T TAKE OFF HIS SEATBELT. Have an adult sit next to him and let him lean on the adult's shoulder.
- Your toddler wants out of his carseat. DON'T TAKE HIM OUT. This is a signal for a toddler to run or time to start a new activity.
- Your infant needs to nurse. DON'T NURSE BABY WHILE DAD IS DRIVING. Stop the car and nurse without risks.
- Your pre-teens want to stretch out in the cargo area of the station wagon. THE CARGO AREA IS FOR CARGO, NOT KIDS.
- Your stubborn five-year-old won't put on his seatbelt. DON'T START DRIVING AWAY. Try offering him a new game or activity as soon as he buckles up. Yelling will just make him more determined.
- Your spouse insists that he is a safe driver and anyway, he drove all over the country as a kid and never wore a seatbelt. DISCUSS THIS BEFORE YOUR TRIP. EXPLAIN HOW IMPORTANT SEATBELTS ARE. IF NOTHING ELSE WORKS, TELL HIM YOU WILL NOT GO UNLESS HE WEARS HIS SEATBELT.

WHAT IF . . . ? TAKE A TRAVEL QUIZ

Are you truly prepared for the problems of car travel? Test yourself. How would you solve these common problems? Circle your correct answer and add your points. Your score will be interpreted at the end of the quiz.

What if your children say:

1. "The sun is still in my eyes!" (And it will be for hours)
   A. Offer the sunglasses you packed. (+3)
   B. Stop the car and let him change seats. (+3)
   C. Suggest child close his eyes and take a nap. (+2)
   D. Turn the car around and change your destination. (−2)

2. "There isn't any toilet paper!" (There had been some but he dropped it onto a very wet floor)
   A. Offer the mini-tissues you always carry. (+3)
   B. Go back to the car for the extra roll of toilet paper packed in the Car Emergency Kit. (+2)
   C. Ask the person in the next stall if you can borrow some toilet paper. (+2)
   D. Sacrifice your handkerchief. (−3)

3. "My crayons keep falling!" (Who let him pack the box with 64 crayons?)
   A. Hook little plastic bags onto car door knobs; tape bags to back of front seat, or pin bags to fabric upholstered seats. (+3)
   B. Use a small box (like a shoe box) that will hold crayons steady. (+2)
   C. Put away all drawing items and start playing "I Spy." (+2)
   D. Hold the crayons and offer them one by one. (−2)

4. "I have to go to the bathroom!" (You're on the expressway and the next rest stop is 35 miles away)
   A. A "necessary jar" or potty with a lid may save the upholstery. (+2)
   B. Ask child to "hold it in." If he claims he'll explode, tell him to "let it out." After one pantswetting episode, he won't complain when you limit amounts of liquids. (−1)
   C. Pull off to the shoulder, position him on the far side of the traffic and let nature take its course. (+1)
   D. Scream, "I told you not to drink your sister's milkshake." (−2)

5. "He's kicking me!" "She won't leave me alone." (It's started already; you are only a half hour from home)
   A. Pull off at the nearest exit or rest stop to switch seats. If possible, have an adult in front and back. (+3)
   B. Pull off at the nearest exit or rest stop for a snack or just to run around. (+3)
   C. Put on your headphones and pretend there is a bullet-proof glass between front and back seat. (−2)
   D. Have a song-fest. (+1)

6. "Here's the box, but I can't find my crayons!" (If the crayon wrappers are there without the crayon inside, you've got troubles)
   A. Scrape the melted crayons off the back seat with your ice scraper. (+2)
   B. Have a mini-science lesson about the effect of a hot sun on a pack of crayons. (+1)
   C. Remember to only take markers on the next trip. (+2)
   D. Scream, "You'll never get another box of crayons in your whole life!" (−3)

7. "I'm going to throw up!" (Next time he won't talk you into ordering him two hamburgers, two order of fries, a large malt and an apple pie)
   A. Hypnotize him by repeating, "You will not, you feel great." (+2)
   B. Hope he aims for the bag you hand him. (+3)
   C. Scream, "If you do, this will be the last trip you'll go on!" (−3)
   D. Gently ask him to lean back and close his eyes and mouth. (+2)

8. "My seatbelt is too tight!" (This is the third time in an hour you've fixed the seatbelt)
   A. Pull off at the nearest exit and change seats; he just needs a new view. (+3)
   B. Start playing his favorite riddle game; he just needs your attention. (+3)
   C. Scream, "I will not! And please stop bothering me!" (−2)
   D. Tell him it will no longer be too tight if he sits up and stops leaning on his sister. (+2)

SCORE

+15 and over

You're an expert. We know you'll have a successful trip.

+9 to +14

OK, so you're not perfect and neither are they. You'll muddle through.

+8 and under

You should reread this chapter. Or—on second thought—are you sure you want to go on this trip?

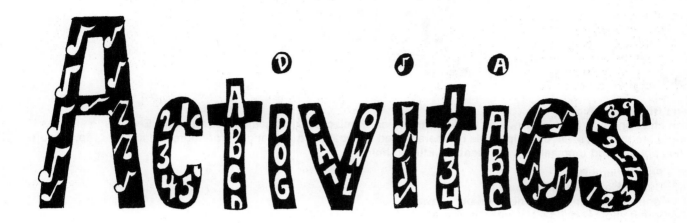

ACTIVITIES

We are not hyperactive cheerleader types who plan every moment of a car trip with our kids. Frankly, we love to sit back and enjoy the scenery, talk over things with our husbands, or just drive without having to talk, think, sing or rhyme.

Yet, we've found that 15 to 20 minutes of activity and interaction with the kids will often result in an equal amount of quiet time when kids will happily occupy themselves.

If you are especially lucky, the car's vibration will lull your kids to sleep. Or, they will become engrossed in their book, in watching the scenery or in a game or activity with their sibling and politely tell you "Turn around, Mom," or "Not now, Dad."

We're sure your family will find a few favorites from our games and activities list. And, hopefully, you'll reach your destination before exhausting every suggestion!

RULES TO REMEMBER

Don't Bring Too Much.
Each child should have his own busy kit with strategically selected toys, games and "lovies." Encourage siblings to coordinate their toys. On one trip, three brothers traded baseball cards off and on for hours. On another trip, two pre-schoolers amused themselves with identical stuffed animals.

Set a Few Ground Rules.
• No loud talking or strange noises.
• Use one toy or game at a time, then put it away.
• Don't use another child's toy without asking.

Select games and toys . . .
• without small pieces (magnetic games are great).
• with versatility (a deck of cards instead of a specific card game).
• that self-store.
• that hold your child's attention.
• that are inexpensive (a bag of plastic dinosaurs, stickers, paper dolls).

Welcome to the Electronic Age!
Some families plug a TV into the cigarette lighter; others travel with personal cassettes, tape recorders and earphones for each child. We enjoy cassette stories, complete with read-a-long books for children. Choose from a variety of tapes: sing-a-long, favorite children's songs, Broadway musicals and educational tapes.

Tapes are worth their investment. Just be ready to listen to the same one over and over. In fact, you'll probably fall asleep singing one of your children's favorite songs.

Save Something for Tomorrow.
If your car trip spans more than one day, save a few suprises for rough times. Have a few inexpensive items wrapped and ready for a long stretch of road.

Pick a Few Toys from Our List:
Magic slates
Electronic games
Action figures
Cassette player, recorder, earphones and tapes
Magnetic games (checkers, bingo)
Favorite dolls
Stuffed animals
Activity and coloring books
Colorforms (they stick to car windows)
Sewing cards
Punch out and lick sticker books
Flashcards
Books
Hand and finger puppets
Little cars and trucks
Question and answer cards from board games
Trading cards
Playing cards
Paper, crayons and markers

OVER 60 IDEAS FOR FAMILY FUN

Car games are the traditional way to pass the time on a car trip. They take our mind off the road and encourage family cooperation and spirit.

As kids, we remember playing "Geography" every summer on our yearly trek East. When we think of the California coast, we recall sing-a-longs and the "A-B-C Sign Game."

As parents, we've become so engrossed in car games with our own family, we've actually missed exits and forgotten scheduled stops.

SET SEVERAL GROUND RULES

1. Never use games when everyone is quietly amusing himself.
2. Never badger drivers into participating, especially during heavy rain or drifting snow.
3. Babies actually like to hear the sounds of the other family members rhyming, guessing, singing and telling stories.
4. Don't worry if the game is too hard for young children. They can participate as team members.
5. Try to play as a group rather than competitively, especially with young children.
6. Beware of keeping track of who wins. Just play for fun.
7. When one game begins falling apart, try another.
8. Scale the game for the age and attention span of your family.
9. Write down funny answers or situations as they happen, in your log pages.
10. Create your own variations on our games to suit your family's interests. Keep track of these variations in your log.

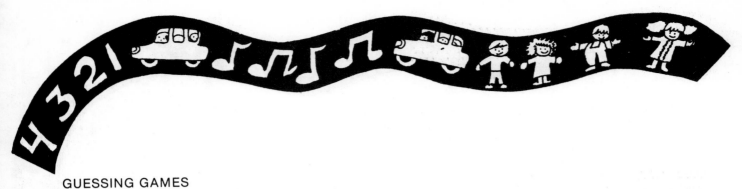

GUESSING GAMES

1. This Guy Is.
  a. First player selects a category such as superhero, rock star, furry creature, sports figure.
  b. Player names the category, and gives two clues.
     "This guy is a superhero. He has red legs, and a black curl on his forehead. Who is he? (answer: Superman)
  c. Allow everyone one guess. If players are stumped, give another clue.
  d. Player who guesses correct answer goes next. If players remain stumped, the present player takes another turn.

2. Alphabet Soup.
  a. First player starts by selecting a word that begins with "A".
  b. Go around the car naming words that begin with the same letter.
     "apple, artichoke, alfalfa."
  c. As soon as a player is stumped, he begins the next alphabet letter.
     "B - bum, blue, boat."
  d. How long will it take your family to complete the alphabet?

3. I Spy.
  a. First player looks carefully around inside the car and selects something.
     (Beware of using outside objects since that brown cow may be two miles away by the time everyone guesses.)
  b. Player gives a color clue. "I spy something green."
  c. Everyone guesses.
  d. Whoever guesses correctly is next. If everyone is stumped, the present player gets another turn.

4. Family Trivia.
  a. First player selects a trivia question relating to the family.
     Think of vacations, friends, pets, and funny family stories.
     (This is also a painless way to review names and identities of friends or relatives you'll be visiting on your trip.)
     "Where were we the last time Craig fell asleep?"
     "What is the name of Aunt Marsha's white poodle?"
  b. Everyone guesses.
  c. Whoever guesses correctly is next. If everyone is stumped, the present player gets another turn.

5. Name That Sound.
  a. First player names an object that has a distinctive sound.
     "Saw" "Clock" "Train"
  b. Other players make the appropriate sounds.
     "BZZZZZZ" "TICK-TOCK" "CHOO-CHOO"
  c. Play this game only if kids are in a cooperative mood. It can easily become a signal for verbal rowdiness!

6. What Am I?
  a. First player selects a category such as a useful object, food, natural wonder, vehicle.
  b. Player names the category and gives two clues.
     "I am a useful object. I have four legs and a flat top. What am I?" (Answer: a table)
  c. Allow everyone two guesses. If players are stumped, give another clue.
  d. Player who guesses, goes next. If players remain stumped, the present player takes another turn.

7. Rhyme Time.
  a. First player chooses a word. "Red"
  b. Each player says a real or make believe word that rhymes with it.
     "led, bed, head, wed."
  c. When players run out of rhymes for that word, they begin a new word.

8. Touch and Tell.
  a. Children close their eyes.
  b. Parents offer objects found in the car or collected at stops.
    (grass, leaves, stones, sticks, wrappers, keys, stuffed animals)
  c. Children guess the objects by touching them.
  d. Reverse the game. Children offer objects for parents to guess.

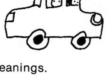

9. Wiggly Words.
  a. First player chooses a word. "Night."
  b. Second player gives the opposite. "Day."
  c. Players work as a team to see how many opposites they can think of.

10. Same Game.
  a. First player chooses a word. "Small."
  b. Each player offers a different word that has the same meaning.
    "little, mini, tiny"
  c. When players are stumped, select another word.

11. Sound Alike Players.
  a. Each player gives a pair of words that sound alike but have different meanings.
    "knight—night" "sun—son" "tail—tale"
  b. Players work together to create as many pairs as possible.

12. Brainstorming.
  a. First player chooses a word. "Red"
  b. Players take turns saying the first thing that pops into their minds.
    "Hearts, fire, cherries, apples, roses, beets, my favorite color."

MEMORY GAMES

13. Potpourri.

  a. First player selects one of these beginnings:
    "I'm going on a trip and in my stationwagon I'm taking..."
    "I ordered a pizza and on it I want..."
    "I want an ice cream sundae with these toppings..."
    "I'm balancing on a tightrope and on my hat I'm holding..."
  b. Then he begins the list. "I'm going on a trip and in my stationwagon I'm taking a banana."
  c. Each player repeats what the others have said, then adds to the list.
  d. When all players have taken a turn or forgot the list, try a new beginning.

14. Identification.
  a. Teach each child his full name, address, and telephone number.
  b. Practice it. Repeat it. Help him memorize it.

15. Geography.
  a. First player selects a place name (city, country, state, river, mountain range, park)
  b. Next player names a place that begins with the last letter of the previous player's word.
    "Amazon River—Redstone Park—Kansas"
  c. Remember what each player has said. Don't repeat the same name.

16. Ghost.

  a. First player has a word in mind. Example: "What"
  b. He begins by saying the first letter "W"
  c. Each player adds a letter, with a real word in mind. "H" ("WHERE")
  d. The object of the game is to avoid completing a word.
  e. Your strategy is to lead other players to complete a word by building a word that has to end on their turn and not on yours.

f. Whoever finishes the word is given one letter to spell the word "GHOST."

g. When one player finishes enough words to have earned the letters, "G-H-O-S-T," he's a "ghost" and the game is over.

Sample game: 1st player says "M" (thinking of "Mane")

2nd player says "E" (thinking of "Men")

3rd player says "T" (by mistake he finishes the word and gets a "G")

The game works better without using two letter words.

FANTASY GAMES

17. Round About Story.
a. First player begins a story. "Once upon a time in a very hilly country, there lived two itsy bitsy, teeny weeny old..."
b. Next player must pick up story and continue.
c. Continue around the car and try to weave a long, intricate, imaginative story.
d. Some families like to tape record this activity and play it back.

18. Make Believe.
a. Each player takes turns responding to these questions:
   If a Martian landed on earth and wanted to know what a child is, what would you say?
   If a wishing tree grew in your yard, what three wishes would you make?
   If you could be an animal, what would you be and why?
   If your tube of toothpaste could speak, what would it say about each family member?
   If you could travel to a far away land, where would you go and why?
   If you won a million dollars, what would you do with it?

19. Family Tales.
a. Tell your favorite fairy tales, but substitute friends and family as the main characters.

20. Magical Toy Box.
a. First player begins, "In my magical toy box I have..." and lists all the very special things and people he loves. "Aunt Nancy's chocolate chip cookies, Uncle Doug's jokes, two real baby-sized dolls, all the candy in the world, Grandma Bessie's soup."
b. Continue until everyone has shared.

21. Sky Shapes
a. Everyone (except the driver!) looks up into the sky and using his imagination, talks about what the clouds look like. "I see a fluffy lamb, a mean dragon..."

22. Inside the House.
a. Be on the lookout for interesting houses or buildings near the side of the road.
b. Make up a story about who lives there. What are their names, ages? occupations? likes and dislikes? What are they doing?

23. Musical Moods.
a. Listen to music on the radio or from a cassette.
b. Based on the mood, sounds or tempo, make up a story. (Classical music works well)

SELF EXPRESSION GAMES

24. Proud as a Peacock.
a. Ask everyone to say something he is proud of about himself. " I can dress myself." "I can play soccer."
b. Ask everyone to list his favorite: color, food, TV show, holiday, cookie, ice cream flavor, friend.

25. You're Terrific.
a. Tell each person in the car something you like about him.
b. Parents should start this one.
c. Keep going until you list several for each person.
   "I like the way Eric always tries to do his best on school tests."
   "I like the way Beth always tells us about her day."

26. Serene Silence.
a. See who can go the longest without making a sound.
b. Give everyone a roll of lifesavers or a bag of jelly beans.
c. Each time he talks, he must give one up!

27. Tell a Dream.
a. Finish the sentence: When I grow up, I'd like to be...
   If I visited outer space, I would...
   If I had a pet, I'd choose a...
   If I could do something very special, it would be...

28. Make a Face Time.
a. Name an emotion. (Surprised, happy, sad, bored, angry, perplexed, jittery, unsure, scared, sly, suspicious)
b. Go around the car and each person makes a face to express that emotion.

29. Share a Feeling.
a. Pick an emotion. (Surprised, frustrated, sad, scared, mad, jealous, happy)
b. Go around the car and each person shares an experience when he felt that emotion.

30. Hand Babies.
a. Pretend your hand is a baby.
b. Name it.
c. Rock it!
d. Teach it a song.
e. Feed and burp it!

31. Herschel.
a. Let your fingers become Herschel or Hershette, a walking, dancing star.
b. Make up songs and dances and take turns performing them.
c. Sometimes Herschel tickles people!

ANIMAL GAMES

32. Animal Sounds.
a. Take turns making animal sounds.
b. Guess the animals.
c. Small kids love this game.
d. Think up exotic animals and their sounds for older kids.

33. Animal Sleuths.
a. First player picks an animal. "Rabbit"
b. He gives two clues. "Long ears, short, fluffy tail"
c. Everyone guesses which animal.

34. Animals on Parade.
a. Count all the living creatures you see as you drive.
   Birds, cows, dogs, cats, horses, iguanas!

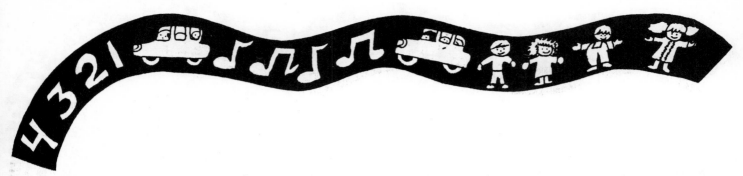

35. Describing Animals.
a. First player says an animal. "Cat"
b. Everyone lists descriptive words that start with the same letter as animal. "curvaceous, cute, cozy, curly, culinary"

36. Rhyming Animals.
a. First player says an animal. "Cat" "Bunny" "Doggy"
b. Other players list descriptive words that rhyme with the animal.
   "Fat cat, funny bunny, soggy doggy"

SINGING GAMES

37. Sing-A-Long.

a. Sing every song you know.
b. Ask kids to teach you their favorite school songs.
c. Teach the kids your high school or college fight song.

38. Hum-A-Long.
a. How many ways can you hum? Laaaalala, leeelleeelee, hoo hoo hoo, ha he he.

39. Pick a Theme.
a. Sing songs with a certain theme. America, flowers, boats, girls' names, nursery rhymes.

40. Old Favorites.
a. "99 bottles of milk on the wall, 99 bottles of milk, If one of those bottles should happen to fall, 98 bottles of milk on the wall."
b. How long will it last?

41. Sing a Story.
a. Make up a tune as you go along.
b. Use the kids' names in it.
c. Sing funny songs about the family.

42. Guess that Tune.
a. Take turns humming a tune.
b. Can anyone guess what song it is?
c. Kids usually love humming their favorite cartoon theme songs.

43. Musical Rounds.
a. Sing songs in a round. "Row-row-row your boat" works well.

44. Copy Cat Claps.

a. First player claps out a rhythm.
b. Can everyone copy it accurately?
c. Make the rhythms progressively harder.

COUNTING GAMES

45. Musical Numbers.
a. Each player puts his hands behind his back.
b. When referee says, "GO," each player brings forward hands with either one, two or no fingers extended.
c. Count all the fingers and then count off among the players.
d. The player the last number lands on is out.
e. Play until all but one player is out.

98

46. Find the Numbers.
  a. Use signs, licenses and billboards to locate numbers from one to 100.

47. Number Rhyme.
  a. Start with "one" and think of rhymes.
  b. Go as far as you can!
     "one - bun" "two - shoe"

48. Odds and Evens.
  a. This is a two player game.
  b. First player selects "odds" or "evens."
  c. Each player puts one hand behind his back.
  d. When the first player says, "one, two, three, shoot," players bring forward their hands with one or two fingers showing.
  e. Add the fingers showing to determine whether the total is odds or evens.
  f. If first player called correctly, he continues to call. If not, second player takes over.

49. Number Facts.
  a. Start at your kids' skill level and make math fun.
  b. Count together. Let kids decide when to stop.
  c. Take turns solving math problems. Let kids give you problems to solve, too.

PENCIL AND PAPER GAMES

These games are great for rest stops, hotels or restaurants, as well as car travel—for anyone able to write and vibrate at the same time.

50. Hand puppets.
  a. Use washable markers or pens to create a puppet on your hand.
  b. Put on puppet shows.

51. Tic Tac Toe.
  a. Teach your kids this classic game.
  b. Don't forget to Meow when it's a cat's game.

52. Silly Circles.
  a. Draw ten circles on a sheet of paper.
  b. Now turn them into ten real or imaginary people or animals.

53. Amazing Scribbles.
  a. Each person draws a scribble on a sheet of paper.
  b. Exchange papers with someone else.
  c. Turn each other's scribbles into funny pictures.

54. Dapper Dots.
  a. Make dots randomly all over a page.
  b. Set a time limit
  c. Connect the dots to make a picture or design.
  d. You don't have to use every dot.
  e. Intricate designs can be colored in with crayons or markers.

55. Alphabet Marathon.
  a. Write the alphabet in a column, one letter to a line.
  b. Write as many words that begin with that letter.
  c. Set a time limit.
  d. For variation, select a category: fruit, famous composers, art supplies.

56. Lengthy List.
  a. List things you might see as you drive:
     telephone pole, signs, cow, fence, barn, yellow car.
  b. Be sure everyone has the same list.
  c. Each time someone sees something on the list, he should cross it off.
  d. The first person who has seen everything on the list is the winner.

57. Alphabet People.
  a. Write the alphabet.
  b. Turn each letter into a letter person.

58. Word Hunt.
  a. Players select a long word: Hamburger, remembrance, gigantic, telephone, etc.
  b. Each person writes the word on the top of his page.
  c. With letters in any order, players find as many small words as possible.
  d. Player with the most words, selects the next long word to work with.

59. Don't Finish the Face.
  a. First player thinks of a word and draws the correct amount of blanks for each letter, putting in one letter as a clue.
  b. First player also draws a big circle that will be the face outline.
  c. Other players try to guess the word by guessing letters.
  d. For every wrong letter, first player draws one feature on the face.
  e. If complete face is drawn before the word is guessed, the first player thinks up a new word and takes another turn.

CAR ACTIVITIES

60. Write a story. Each child writes for a certain amount of time and then reads his story to everyone.

61. Read a book to the kids, one chapter at a time. Set up specific times for reading.

62. Silent reading. Everyone reads his own book.

63. Talk-a-Day. Review the day's activities with the kids. Where are you going? Where will you be tomorrow?

64. Trace the route. Give each kid a map and a marker. Show him how to trace the route and read a map.

65. Family Photothon. Look through family pictures and talk about the relatives you'll be visiting.

66. Plan-a-Day. Read through tour books and each person plans a special day's activities.

67. Scribe. Together write in the Daily Log. Think up funny things you want to remember.

HURRAY! WE'RE HERE!

The hours of driving have paid off. We arrive at our destination. Toys are restuffed into Busy Kits. Super snack trash is tossed out. The family unbends and emerges from the car. Adults stretch, congratulating themselves on a drive that wasn't so bad after all. Kids look around, eagerly anticipating the adventures to come.

Before sight seeing or visiting family, take time to dig in and get settled.

STAKE OUT YOUR SPACE

- Announce the sleeping arrangements or ask for requests. Who will share the queen size bed? Who will sleep on the cot?
- Give everyone a place for his clothes, personal possessions and toys. Kids love having their own drawers or desks. The hotel room will stay neater if everyone knows where to put dirty clothes, toys, backpacks, coats, food, toothbrushes.
- Set up the bed for a young child, so he'll look forward to his nap or bedtime. Put out his favorite stuffed animal.
- Wander around the room with the kids. Find the bathroom, light switches, windows, doors, dresser, television. Let the kids become familiar with the room, while you scout out possible dangers (lamp cords, exposed plugs, sharp edges, complimentary matches).
- Rearrange the room to suit your needs. Set up a barrier between your bed and the baby's crib, create a corner where toddler can play safely.

101

TAKE TIME OUT

- Kids play quietly, watch TV.
- Adults close their eyes for a short time.
- Pull out tour books and yellow pages and make a few preliminary phone calls.
- Gather together your swimsuits and gear. Relax in the hotel pool.
- Wander around the hotel together.

SET BASIC RULES

- Never open the door to the hotel room.
  (Young children may think the hallway is an extension of their room.)
- Speak softly and walk quietly.
  (Show the kids that there are other rooms on your floor and explain, "other hotel guests might be sleeping, and can hear you when you cry or scream...")
- In case of fire, do not open the door and do not use the elevator.
  (Read over the fire exit instructions and show the kids where the stairwell is.)
- Don't hide anything under the beds or throw around your toys. We're not at home!

GET YOUR BEARINGS

"Case out the joint" together with this exploring game. Who can find the...
- Pop machine
- Ice machine
- Snack machine
- Video games
- Swimming pool
- Restaurants
- Coffee Shop
- Gift Shop
- Front door
- Most comfortable chair in the lobby
- Nearest restrooms to the pool
- Reservation desk
- Elevators

Orient the kids by asking them the following questions:
- What city are we in?
- What's the name of our hotel?
- What street is it on?
- What floor are we on?
- What floor is our room on?
- What is our room number?

Scribing

SCRIBING

"We'll never forget that!" we say after watching our kids' funny shenanigans and hearing their memorable comments during our travels.

"We've got to tell the Halls about that terrific restaurant with the homemade cinnamon-raisin bread," we vow.

Yet, once home, after the first few tellings, we stow away our stories with our gear. Details fade and are replaced by fresh experiences.

Here is an opportunity to store all of that wonderful information. The daily log sheets offer you a place to record the details of your trip.

You'll remember how three year old Garrett stuck his head through the bars of the sea lion's tank and remained stuck while the sea lion swam in for a closer inspection...how disoriented, four-year-old twins, arriving at a large hotel late at night, got out of the elevator and, looking around at the hallway close to our room, said, "Where will we hang our clothes?" "Where are the beds?"

You'll have a record of all the special places you just happened upon: the neighborhood diner with the imaginative, healthy lunches, the perfumerie, hidden on a street of look-alike houses, the well-equipped playground, in the midst of a quiet neighborhood. You'll be able to return and enjoy these spots once more, or recommend them to friends.

Scribing should be enjoyed together as a family. Share the space with your children's writing and their drawing. Reread the previous day's entry to the kids during a quiet time.

Most of all, record the little pleasures, the silly moments, the inappropriate comments, the incredible mix-ups. Years from now this log will bring back delightful memories.

HOW TO USE THE LOG PAGES

- **APPROACH THE LOG IN YOUR OWN INDIVIDUAL STYLE.**
  Write daily entries, keep up a flowing commentary of trip bits and pieces, jot down addresses, directions and phone numbers. Make notes on the trip's progress—what works, what you'll do differently next time. Keep track of the items you wish you had brought.

- **ASK EACH FAMILY MEMBER TO PARTICIPATE**
  How did he feel about the day's adventure?
  What was the best part of the day?
  Name one thing he enjoyed.
  Share something he'd like to do again.
  What was the silliest, funniest, scariest, most surprising or most interesting event?

- **ASK OLDER CHILDREN TO WRITE THEIR OWN LOG.**
  Hand them pencil and paper, or better yet, their own notebook.
  Include their log within the family log pages once you're home.

- **DESIGNATE A TIME EACH DAY FOR LOG WRITING AND READING.**
  At bedtime, write about today, review yesterday, and talk about tomorrow. Tuck your log and a pen into your daily travel bag and take advantage of waiting time, at restaurants, amusement parks, shows.

- **OFFER CHILDREN PAPER TO DRAW ABOUT THEIR DAILY ACTIVITIES**
  Draw the scenery, your dinner, the people you met, the funniest part of your day, an exciting moment, yourself. Include their drawings in your log once you're home.

HINT: Offer paper to children on the spot. We've had our kids sketch pigeons at a fountain, sharks in a tank and Indian masks in a showcase.

This is the story of the _____ family's
                                    (FAMILY NAME)

trip to _____
                        (DESTINATION)

We begin this journey on _____
                                              (DATE)

Those hearty souls who are traveling together include:

_____

_____

_____

_____

Our address at home is: _____
                               (NUMBER)   (STREET)

_____
         (CITY)   (STATE)

Our telephone # is: _____

Along the way we hope to:

_____

_____

_____

_____

We left at _____ o'clock. We planned to leave at _____

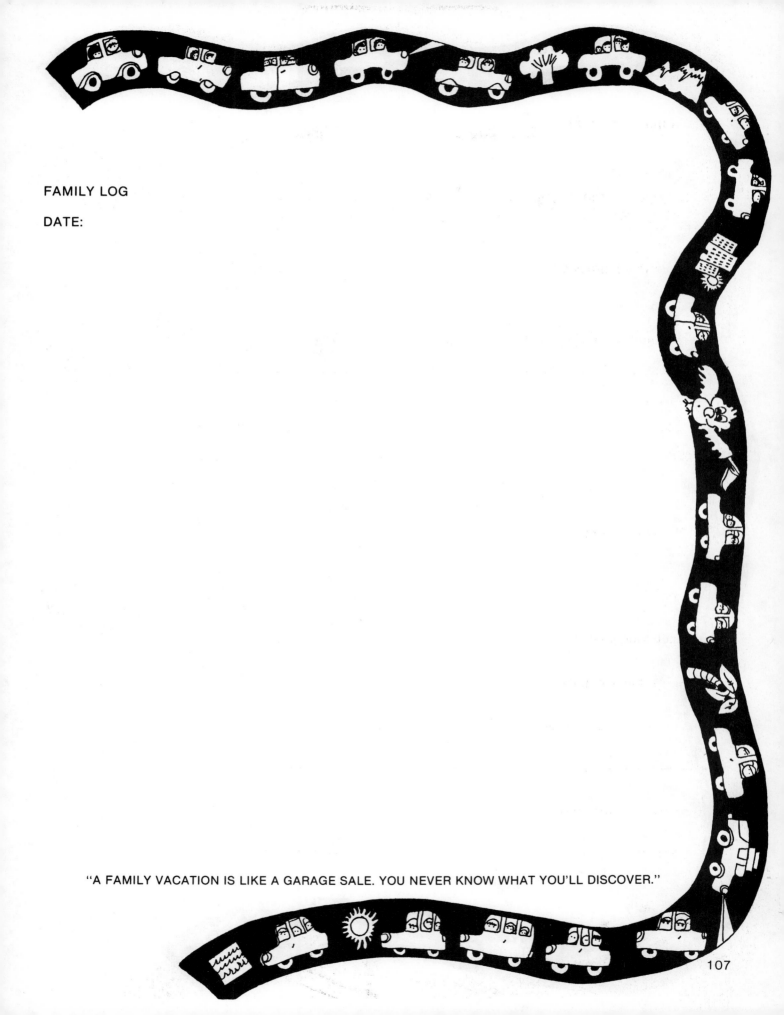

FAMILY LOG

DATE:

"A FAMILY VACATION IS LIKE A GARAGE SALE. YOU NEVER KNOW WHAT YOU'LL DISCOVER."

FAMILY LOG

DATE:

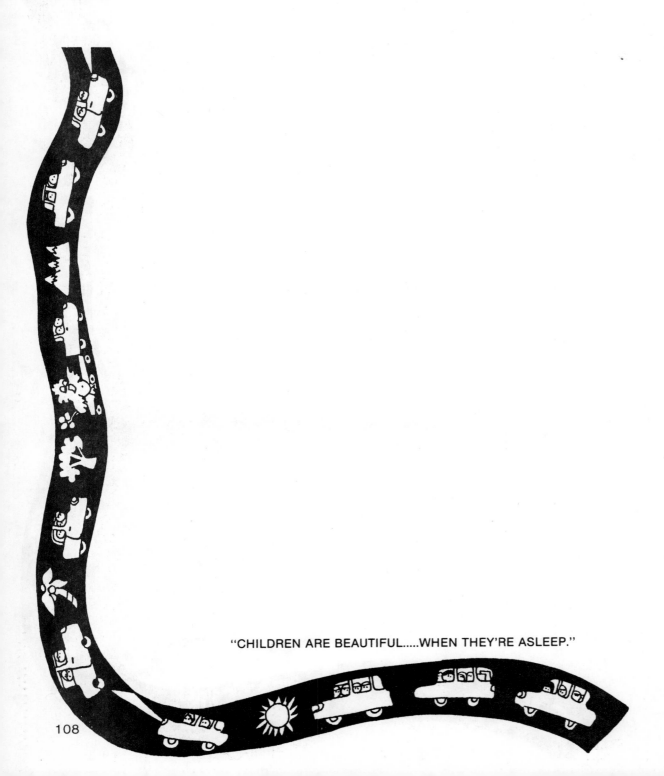

"CHILDREN ARE BEAUTIFUL.....WHEN THEY'RE ASLEEP."

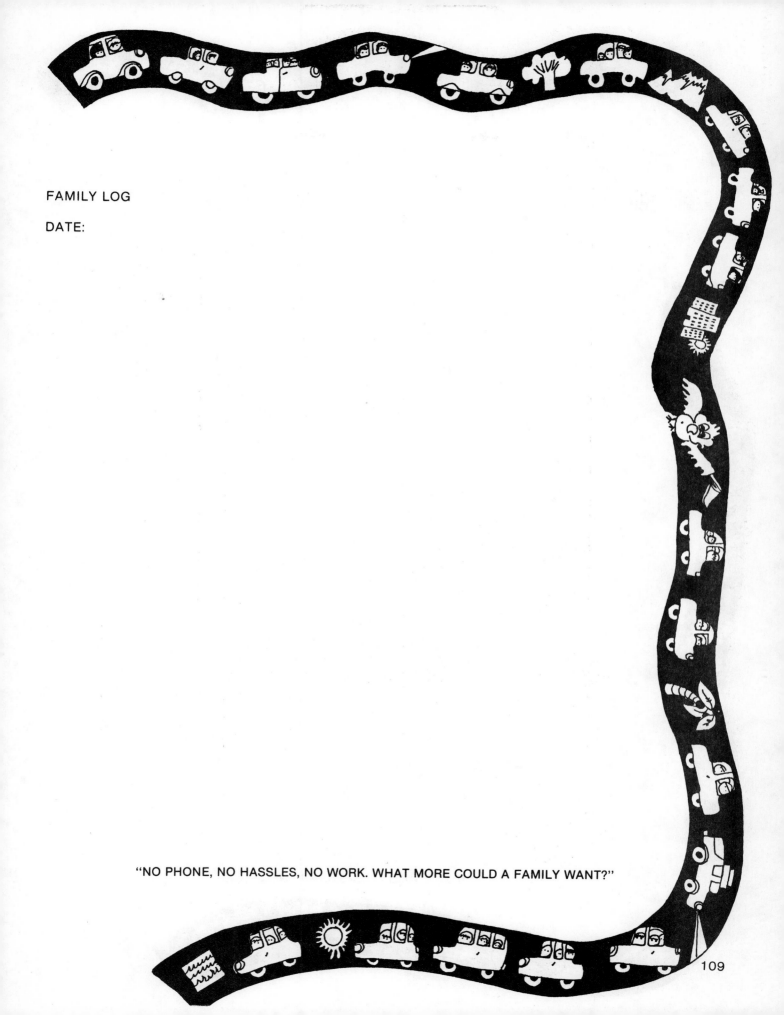

FAMILY LOG

DATE:

"NO PHONE, NO HASSLES, NO WORK. WHAT MORE COULD A FAMILY WANT?"

FAMILY LOG

DATE:

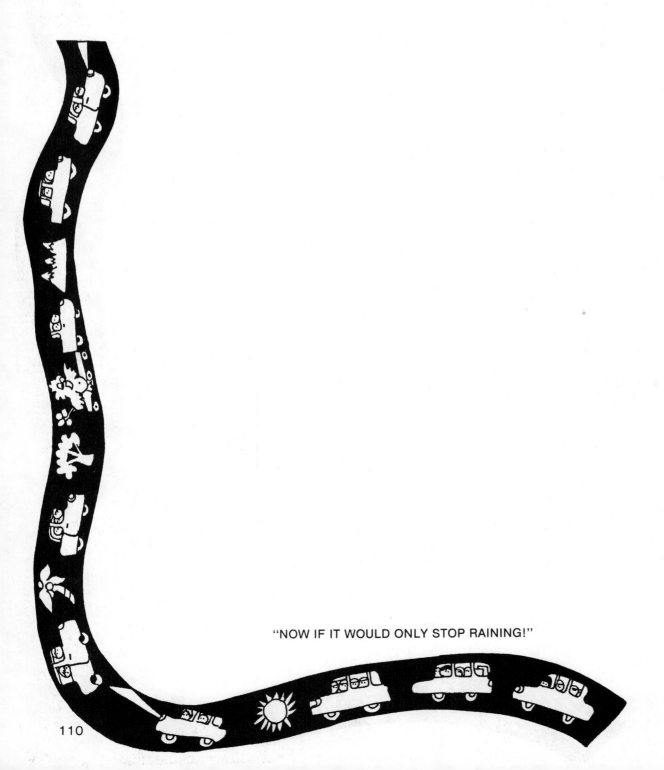

"NOW IF IT WOULD ONLY STOP RAINING!"

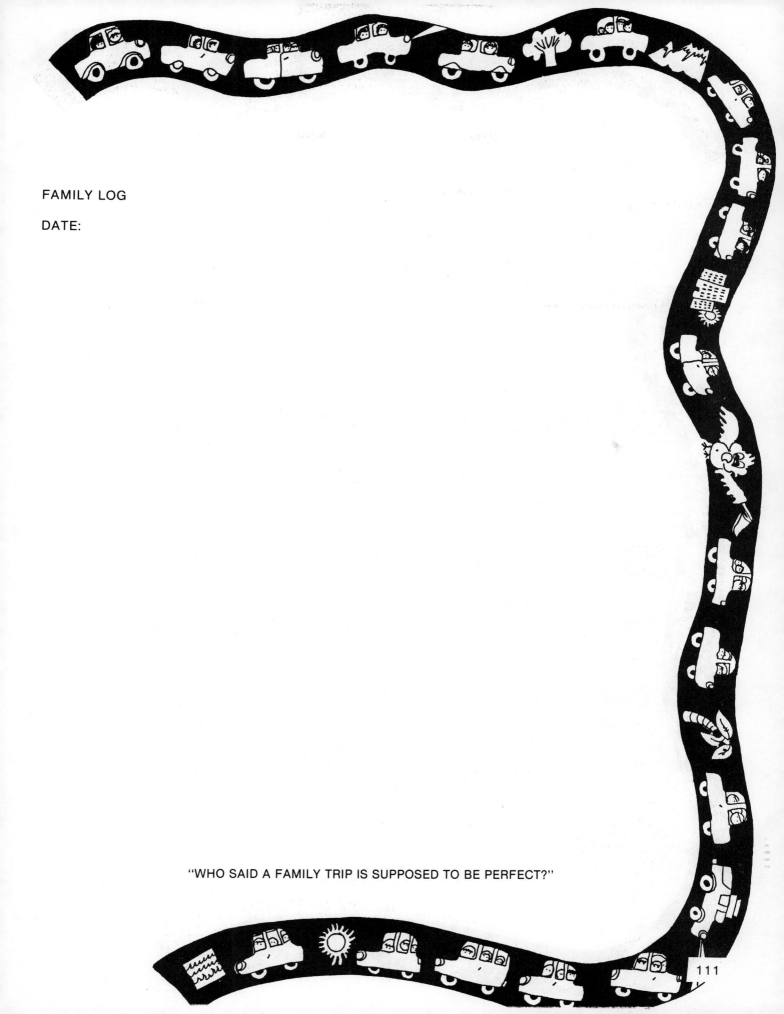

FAMILY LOG

DATE:

"WHO SAID A FAMILY TRIP IS SUPPOSED TO BE PERFECT?"

FAMILY LOG

DATE:

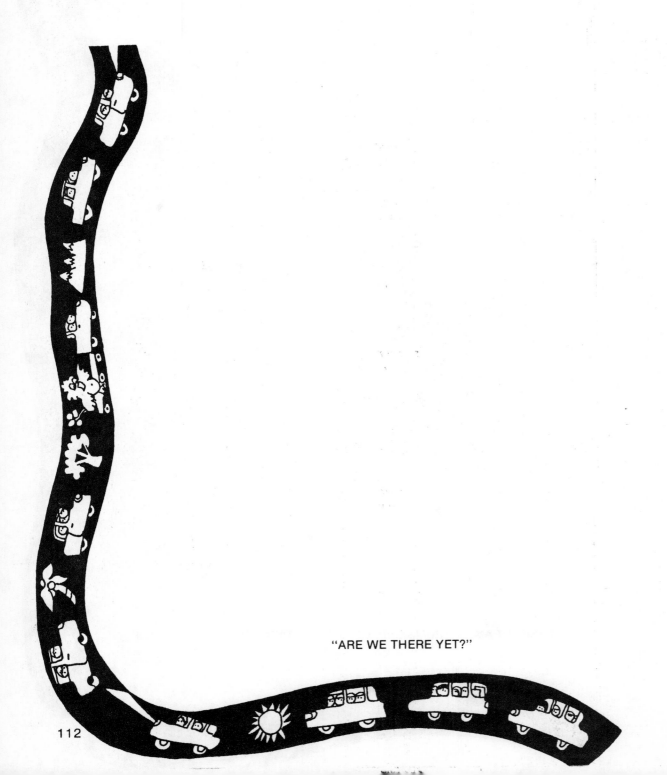

"ARE WE THERE YET?"

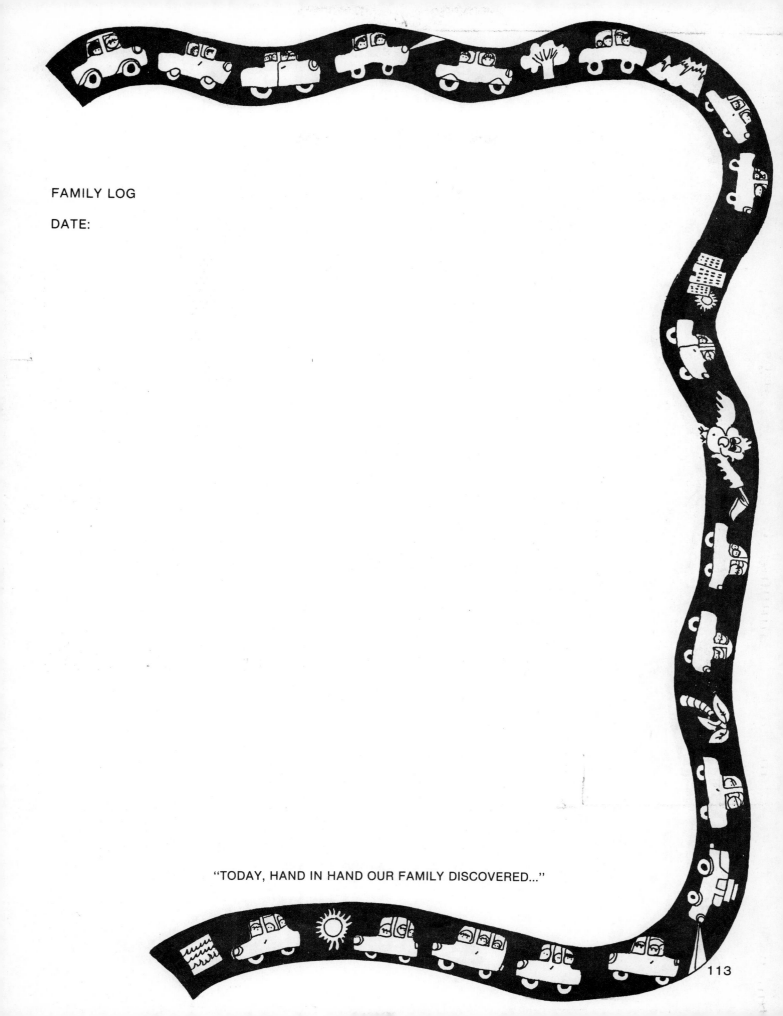

FAMILY LOG

DATE:

"TODAY, HAND IN HAND OUR FAMILY DISCOVERED..."

FAMILY LOG

DATE:

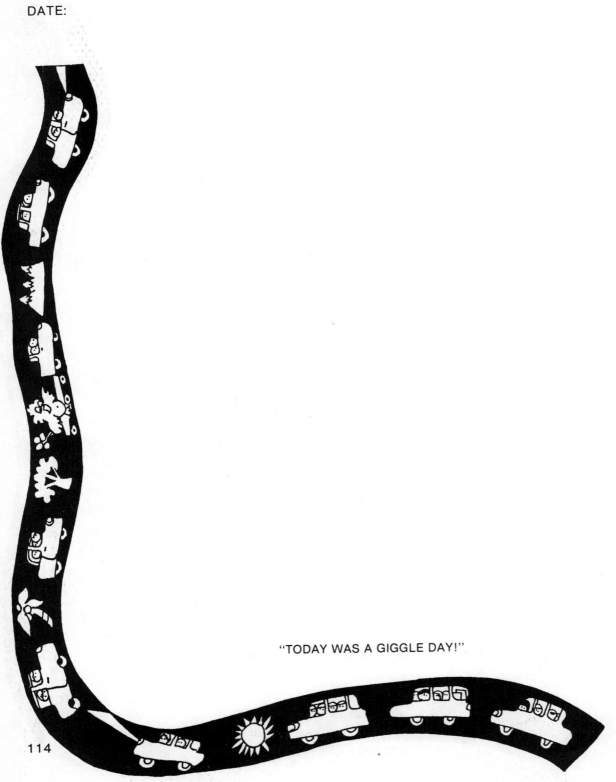

"TODAY WAS A GIGGLE DAY!"

114

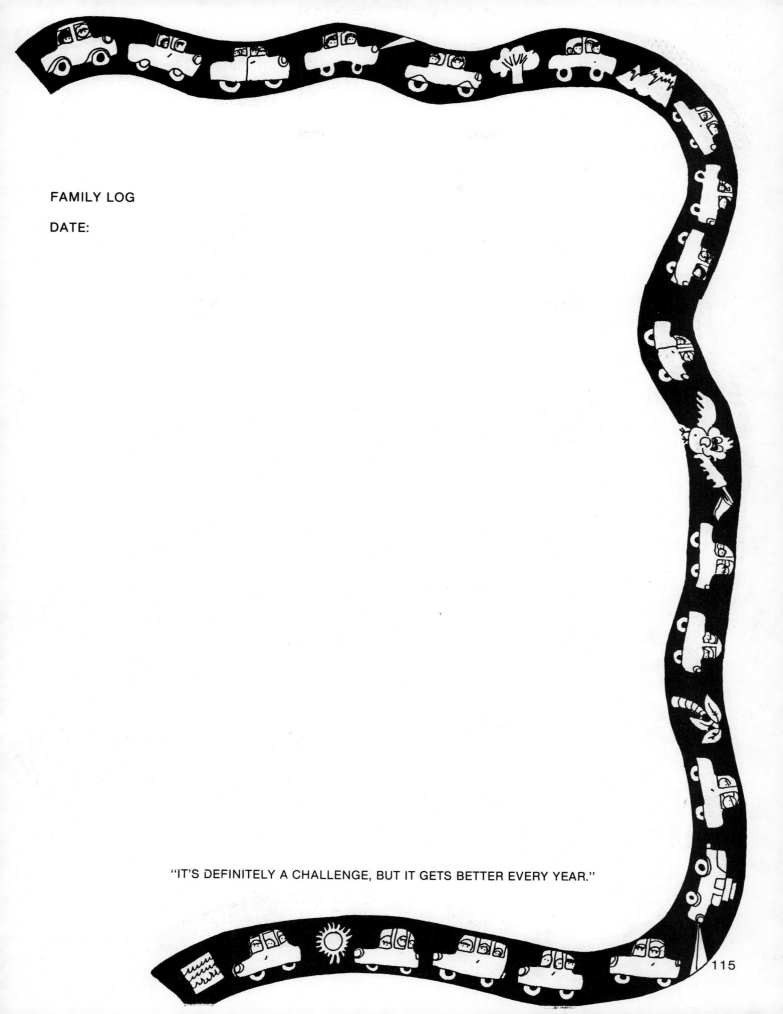

FAMILY LOG

DATE:

"IT'S DEFINITELY A CHALLENGE, BUT IT GETS BETTER EVERY YEAR."

FAMILY LOG

DATE:

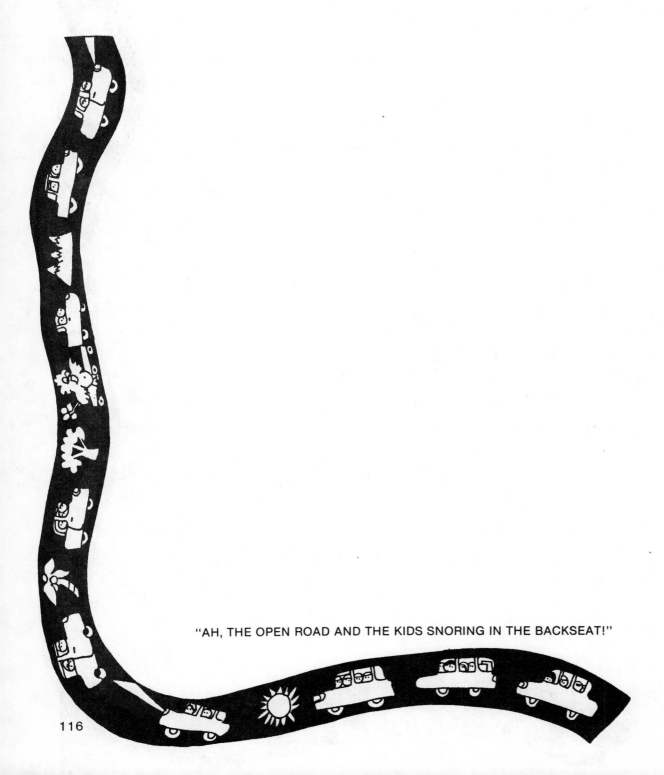

"AH, THE OPEN ROAD AND THE KIDS SNORING IN THE BACKSEAT!"

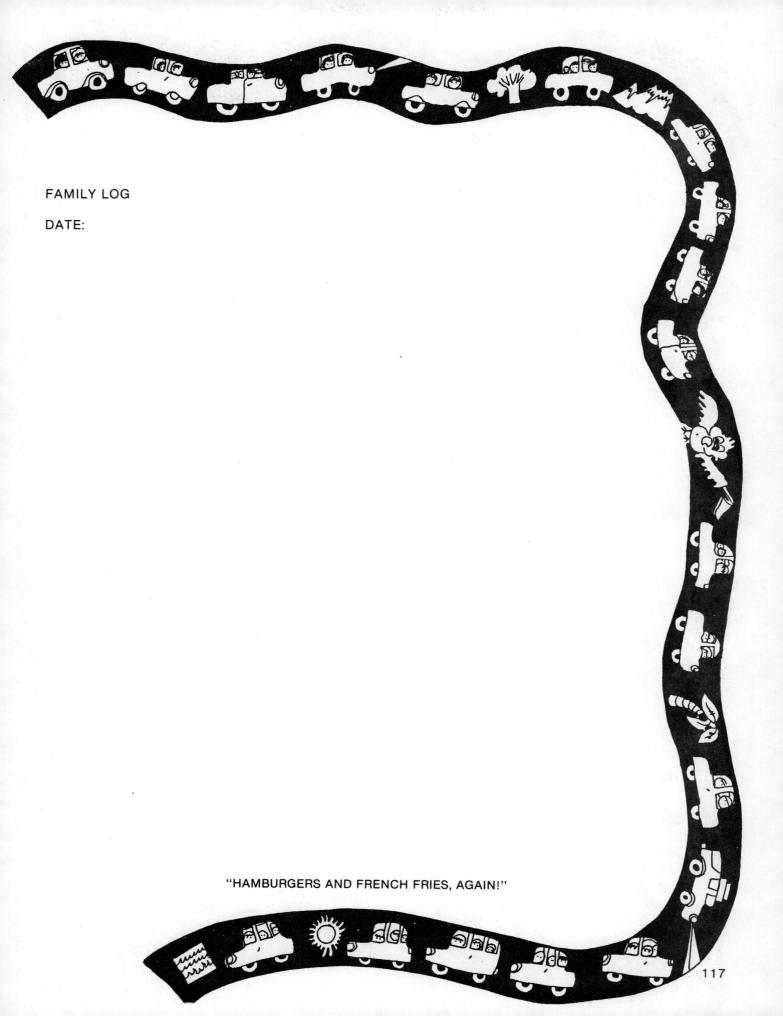

FAMILY LOG

DATE:

"HAMBURGERS AND FRENCH FRIES, AGAIN!"

FAMILY LOG

DATE:

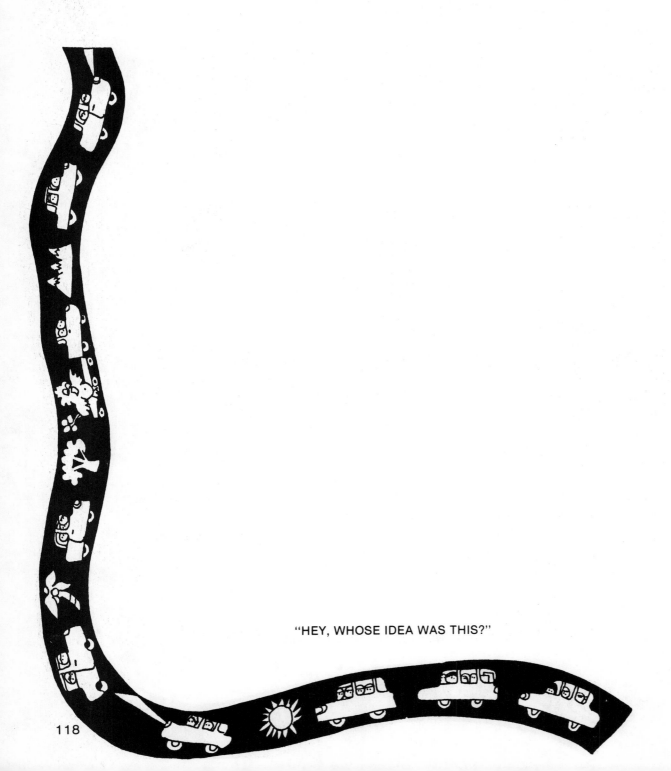

"HEY, WHOSE IDEA WAS THIS?"

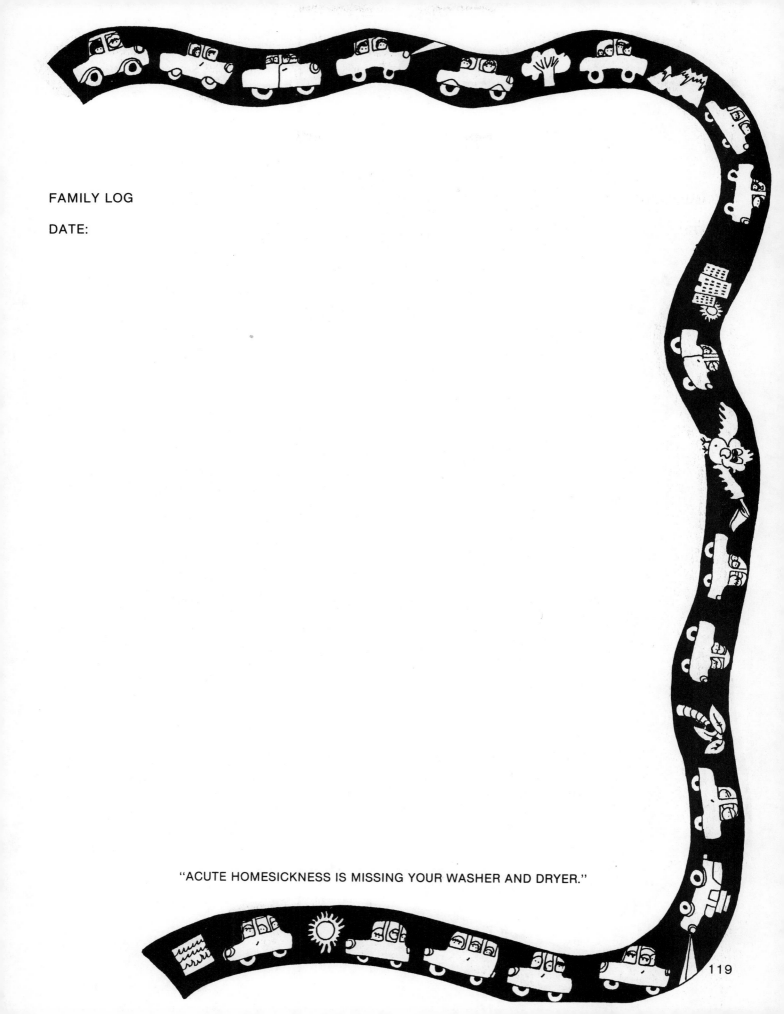

FAMILY LOG

DATE:

"ACUTE HOMESICKNESS IS MISSING YOUR WASHER AND DRYER."

FAMILY LOG

DATE:

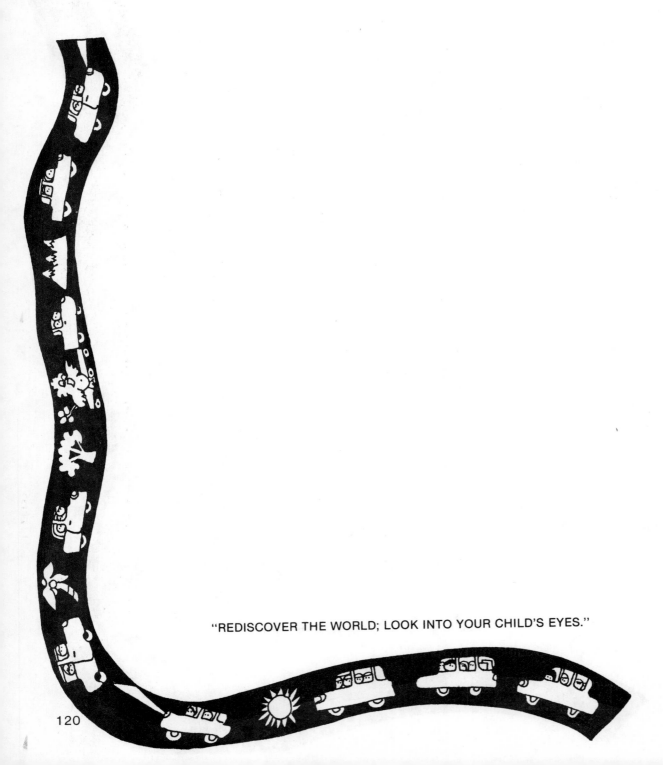

"REDISCOVER THE WORLD; LOOK INTO YOUR CHILD'S EYES."

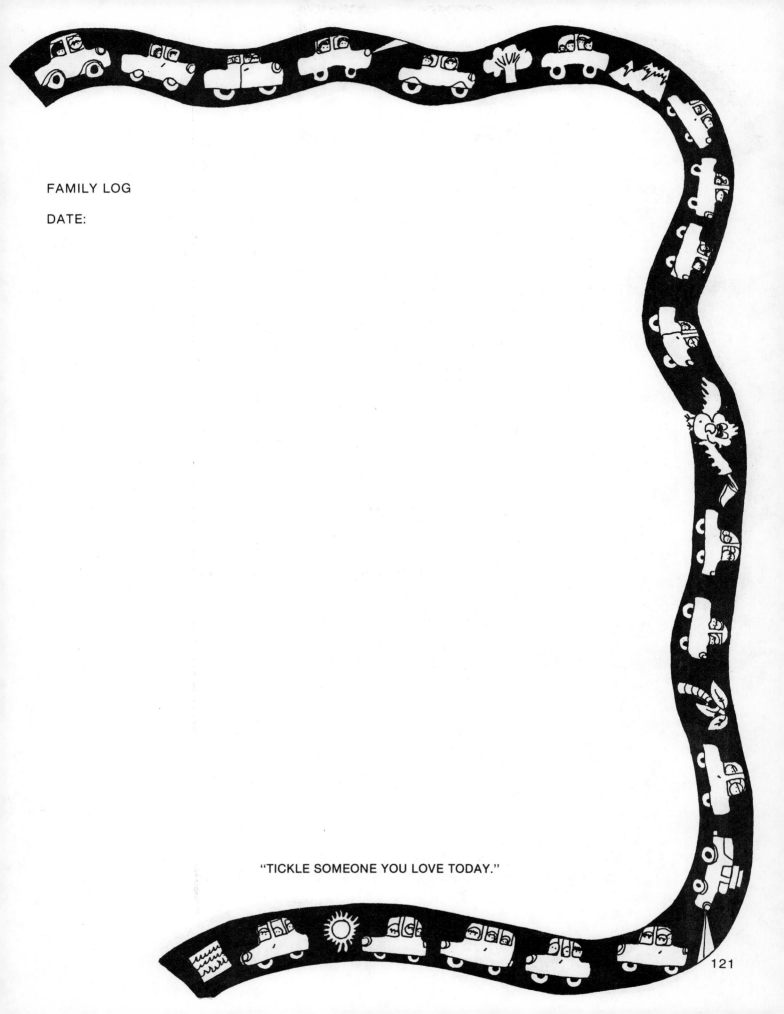

FAMILY LOG

DATE:

"TICKLE SOMEONE YOU LOVE TODAY."

FAMILY LOG

DATE:

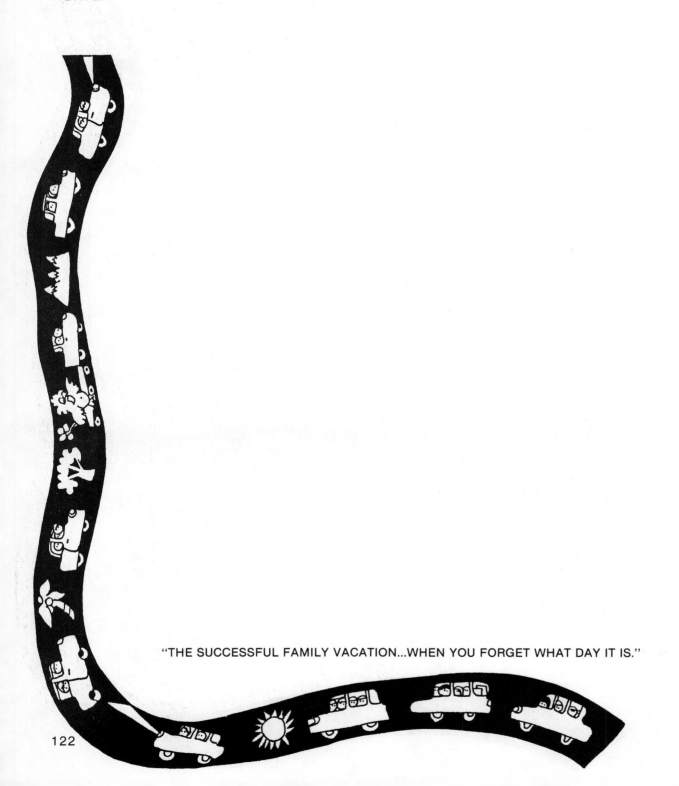

"THE SUCCESSFUL FAMILY VACATION...WHEN YOU FORGET WHAT DAY IT IS."

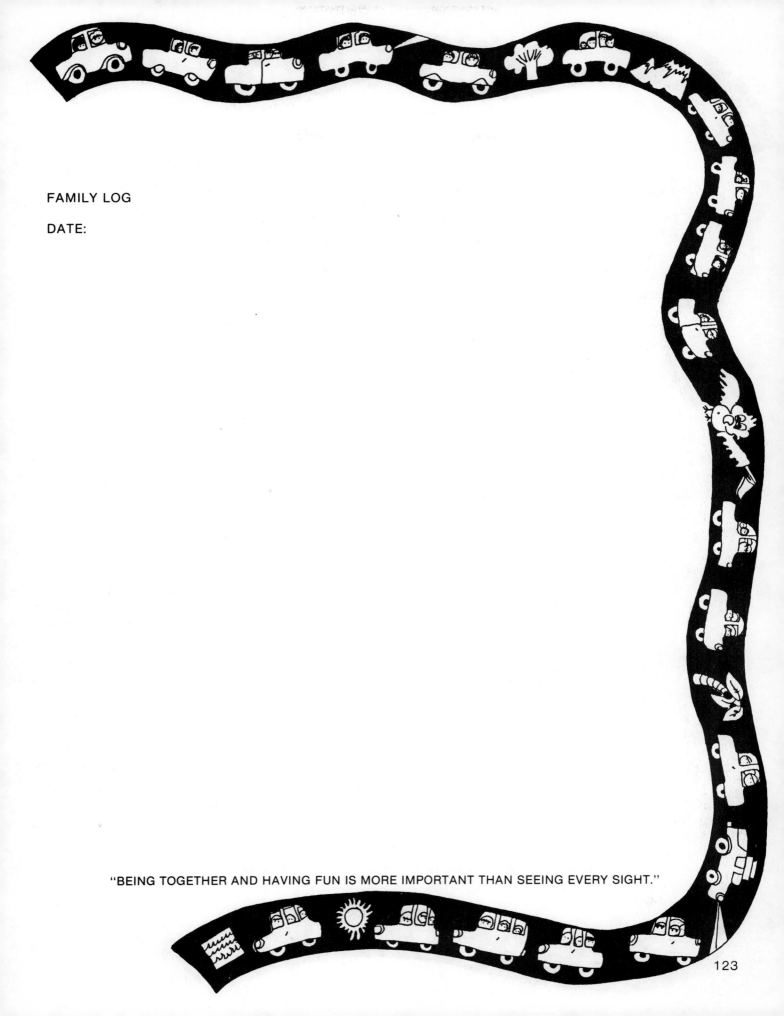

FAMILY LOG

DATE:

"BEING TOGETHER AND HAVING FUN IS MORE IMPORTANT THAN SEEING EVERY SIGHT."

FAMILY LOG

DATE:

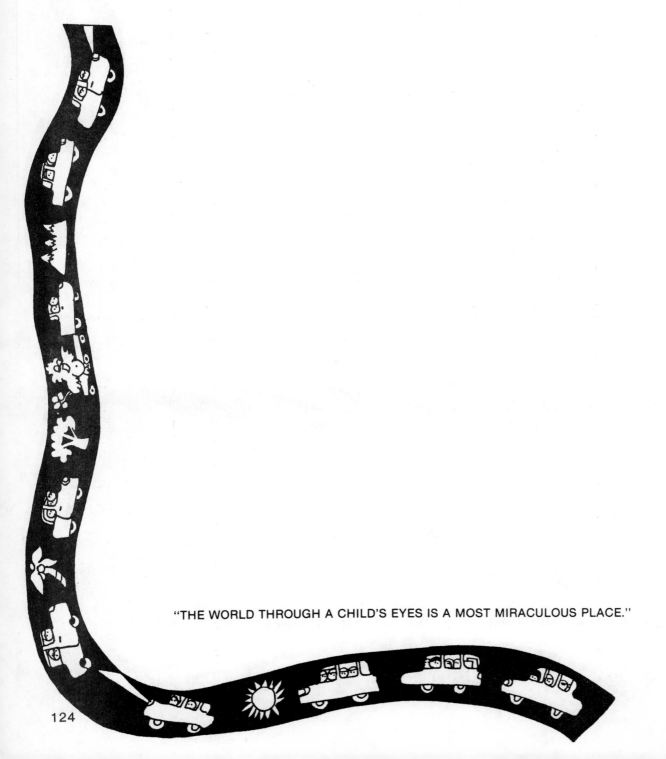

"THE WORLD THROUGH A CHILD'S EYES IS A MOST MIRACULOUS PLACE."

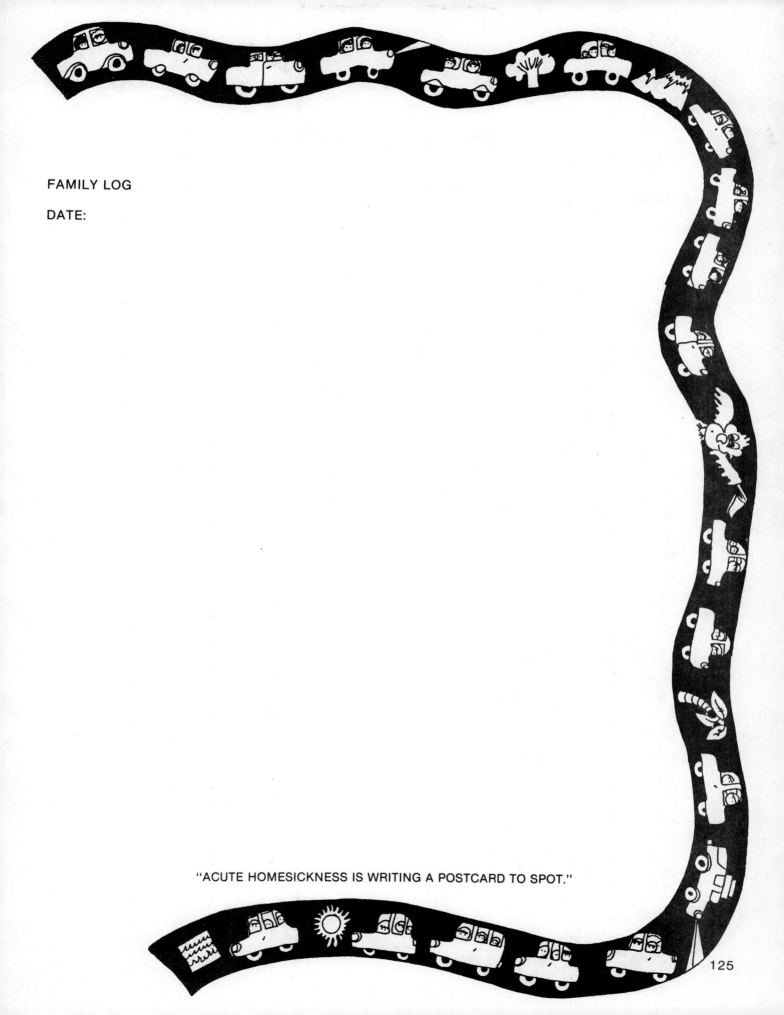

FAMILY LOG

DATE:

"ACUTE HOMESICKNESS IS WRITING A POSTCARD TO SPOT."

FAMILY LOG

DATE:

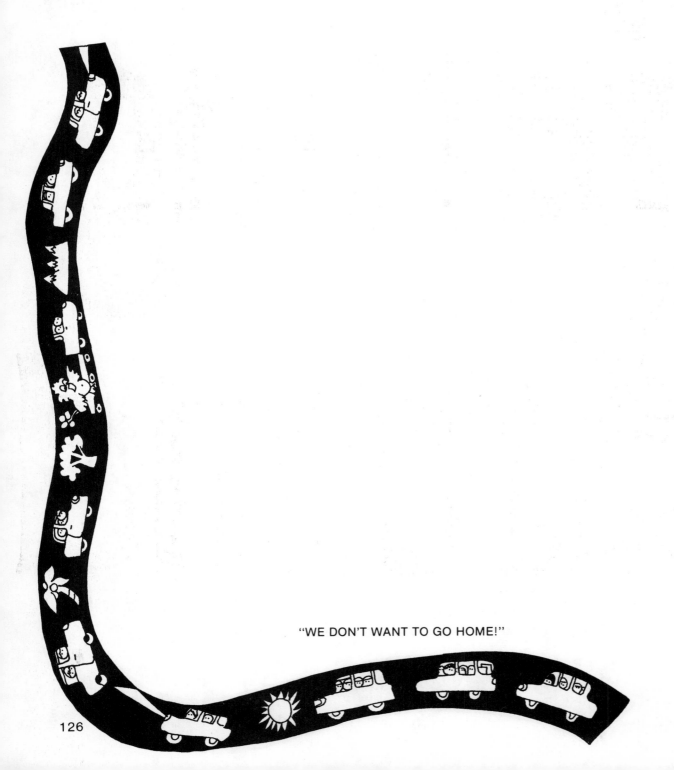

"WE DON'T WANT TO GO HOME!"

Getting Around

WP

PLACES

So much to see, so much to do and so little time. Tour books and brochures beckon us onward.

Without using caution and restraint, we would wear out our family in just one morning. So we carefully plan the places we visit and alternate the types of restaurants we frequent. We adjust to the needs of the situation, constantly reminding ourselves there is always tomorrow.

Planning

Some attractions that sound tempting may end up being expensive wastes of time. We've fallen prey to many glossy pamphlets, paid exorbitant entrance fees and once on the other side of the turnstile, found ourselves in a run down, deserted attraction complete with out-of-order signs.

Yet, even in the worst kept attractions, if we keep our grumbling to a minimum, the kids will always find something that excites them.

Our children still talk about one summer's visit to a prehistoric dinosaur park. The dinosaurs were rain worn, messy looking affairs with bare wire patches where fake fur had fallen off. The price of admission was to include a "train back millions of years into the dense primordial forests of prehistoric beasts." The pamphlet didn't mention that the ride took less than five minutes, the dinosaurs didn't move because they were broken and the tour guide, who walked us through the "forest," could barely remember his memorized speech. Yet the kids were mesmerized and overwhelmed. They couldn't believe their good fortune—to be so close to such savage looking dinosaurs!

We strongly recommend calling the attraction from your hotel when you first arrive, to confirm your information and help plan when to schedule your visit.

SIGHT CALLING GUIDE

BE SURE TO ASK ABOUT...

Admission Price
- Family package?
- Weekend package?
- Holiday package?
- Discounts? Coupons?
- What does the admission price include?
- Are there additional costs? (such as special shows, exhibits, rides)
- Parking costs?

Hours
- Daily times?
- Weekend times?
- Holiday closings?
- When is it the least crowded?
- Do any areas or special rides close early?

Amenities
- Types of food available?
- Restaurants on the premises?
- Stroller rental?
- Special attractions for specific age group? (toddler rides, teenage or adult rides)

Location/Directions
- How long should it take to get there from your hotel?
- How much time is recommended to completely see this sight?

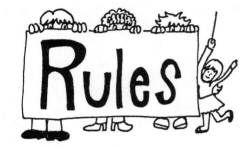

RULES TO REMEMBER

1. Make it cost effective.
Don't go to a high admission sight unless you can spend the day, the weather promises to be right and the kids will have the stamina and capacity to enjoy themselves.

2. Change plans mid-stream.
Don't be afraid to scrap the day's plan, if it isn't working. Kids' needs and schedules must take precedence over your itinerary.

If the baby "wants out" and the toddler "wants up," the art museum may not be much fun. Go straight to the nearest county park and let the kids play in the sandbox all afternoon.

3. Save something for next time.
You don't have to see everything this visit. The kids might actually enjoy a relaxing-go-nowhere day at the hotel—exploring, swimming, playing video games, and snacking at the coffee shop.

Or, try an activity that you never seem to find time for at home, like miniature golf or bowling.

4. Schedule afternoon rest and relaxation.
Kids (and parents!) tire easily in strange environments, especially with different bedtimes and schedules. Try to wind down every afternoon with a nap or quiet play.

While younger children and Mom or Dad nap, older children can watch cartoons, have a snack, read, play games or write in their log.

5. Schedule Run-Around Time.
Kids need time for outdoor play. Find a plaza, park, playground, beach, university campus, or boardwalk and let them yell, run, play tag and act like kids. We try to do this at least once a day.

SIGHT SURVIVAL GUIDE

We seem to visit at least one of these attractions on every trip. We're getting better at it.

THEME PARK

1. If possible, go when the park is least busy, on the off-season, during the week, or on a holiday. (We found Disneyland an uncrowded pleasure on the day of Christmas Eve.)

2. If you must go on a weekend, during peak season, prepare the kids ahead of time to expect crowds, lines and waiting. Come equipped with patience, treats and lots of distracting imagination games.

3. Use a stroller with an attached bag. Even three-year-olds who usually hate strollers will be happy to have a ride as the day wears on. The stroller bag will save your arms some stress. (Most parks rent strollers.)

4. Bring the Day Trip Kit. It includes almost everything you could possibly need. You will be glad to have a change of clothing, sweaters, straws and cups.

5. Dress appropriately. Low, comfortable shoes for everyone (even moms). Jackets and sweaters are a must—rides will make you feel chilly even on sunny days. Hats for baby and toddler on sunny days—winter or summer.

6. Save money by bringing snacks or a bag lunch. Some parks have locked spaces to store your picnic until you're ready for it.

7. Set limits for the amount of money that will be spent on extras like souvenirs, toys, snacks and video games. Our kids always know ahead of time how many surgary treats they can have and how much they can spend on souvenirs.

HINT: Always buy your souvenirs and toys at the end of the day. Otherwise, you'll have more to carry and keep track of. The kids will be kept busy all day, thinking about their future purchases, every time they pass a vendor or display.

8. Take a few breaks. Don't worry if you don't get to every ride. If the kids are exhausted, you should stop for a snack or a meal, or just leave for a good night's sleep.

MUSEUMS

1. Make a bargain with the kids. Let them choose one museum they're anxious to visit (wax, dinosaur, fire engine, space, hands-on, plantetarium, aquarium) and then you pick the museum you're excited to visit (modern art, historical, folk crafts, Asian art).

   Share the excitement with each other!

2. Explain museum rules beforehand. Talk softly, keep together, no running, no touching.

3. Never try to see every exhibit in large musuems. Pick the few exhibits, rooms or floors your kids will enjoy. Spend lots of time there.

4. Allow the kids active expression as they walk through the museum:

Museum Treasure Hunt

Choose several things to look for: shapes, colors, pictures of children, animals, boats, or monsters.

For older kids, make a list of items they might see and have them check each off as you walk through.

Museum Acting

Stop in front of a painting, sculpture, or stuffed bird and assume that pose or expression. Once they get the hang of it, kids love this. It makes the exhibits come to life.

Museum Sketching

Sit down on the floor or on a bench in front of the masks, puppets or modern art, pull out sketch pads and crayons. Kids love trying to copy what they see and you'll have a great record of the trip.

5. Take time out for a special treat. Lots of museums have made their cafeterias appealing places and offer a large selection of foods. Kids love walking through a cafeteria line and choosing special treats.

6. Ask at the information desk if there are highlights for children that shouldn't be missed: special hidden stairways, outdoor sculpture gardens, daily concerts, films, moveable exhibits, and the classic exhibits that kids adore: puppets, masks, mummies and dragons.

7. Use a stroller with an attached bag for three-year-olds and under.

8. Limit the amount of money spent at the gift shop.

SHOPPING MALLS/LARGE DEPARTMENT STORES

1. If you are traveling during major holidays, a trip to the mall is mandatory. Count it as an exciting, leisurely activity rather than a chore.

2. Notice store windows and special exhibits, free concerts and promotional activities.

3. Between shopping, visit the departments kids will love:
   - **Specialty Foods:** Smell the coffees and freshly baked cookies, count the number of pasta shapes, watch the lobsters and drool over the chocolates. Buy something for later!
   - **Office Supply:** For $1.00 or less, kids can buy stickers and stars. They can try out computers and markers.
   - **Audio-Visual:** Kids love watching the same show simultaneously on 15 different televisions screens.
   - **Furniture:** Rest for a few minutes on the chairs or couches.
   - **Pets:** Can you name all the exotic reptiles and birds? Which would you like to own? Buy a present for Spot.
   - **Toys:** We save this for last. It's hard for little ones to look but not touch and we always end up dragging them away, crying over the toys they wish we would buy. Don't be afraid to say "NOT TODAY!"

4. Strollers are mandatory for three-year-olds and younger. (Some malls rent them.)

5. Attach a large bag to the stroller to stash all the goodies.

6. If your kids are too old for a stroller, still bring along a large bag to carry coats, gifts and purchases.

THE WALKING TOUR: AN ALMOST FREE FAMILY ACTIVITY

Walking tours are a terrific family activity, an adventure full of small pleasures and exciting finds, a way to familiarize yourself with your new environment and best of all...they are unstructured and relatively low cost.

Be Sure To Have:
- Comfortable shoes
- Backpack or stoller bag to free your arms
- Stroller or carrier for three-year-olds and under
- Small, lightweight blanket
- Day Trip Kit
- Crayons, paper and reading books for all ages
- Camera
- A good sense of direction or a trusty map

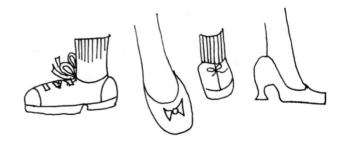

Be Sure To:

Break up the walk by stopping frequently to snack, browse, shop, take photos, play and picnic.

Give your stroller-bound kids time to climb out and stretch, walk a bit and run around. (Tire them out for an afternoon nap!)

Find a grassy park, campus commons, secluded beach or city square. Spread out the blanket and collapse. The kids can lie on their backs and study the clouds while you change baby's diaper. Pass out the snacks while everyone is reading, coloring or watching the scenery or people.

Make the walking tour come alive. Tune the kids into VISUAL EXCITEMENT.

Look For:
- **Reflections:** Kids love skipping ahead of their shadows, seeing themselves reflected in store windows, watching wiggly images in puddles and oil slicks. Look up to see the magic reflections of high tech glass buildings. Murals or adjacent buildings will often be reflected as mirror images.
- **Colors:** Wear "magic glasses" and everything around you will be a blaze of color. Find red tile roofs, blue irises, black grill work, lime green and purple houses, white fences and pink apple blossoms. Be color sleuths. Can the kids find six shades of green? Are certain store windows arranged by color? Can anyone find a turquoise car? A cranberry flag? A yellow flower?
- **Shapes:** Rectangles, cylinders, circles, squares, and triangles are all around us. Can the kids find them in buildings, shrubbery, houses, and signs? Be on the lookout for arches, crescents and curlicues hidden in the trim of house moldings, roofs and windows. Find the carved monsters, animals and gargoyles hidden in old buildings' ornamental work. Track down outdoor sculpure. Walk around it and view it from many angles.

THREE WALKING TOURS

You're the boss. How long, how leisurely the walking tour depends on your family. Maybe you'll find an interesting spot and spend the day there. Maybe you'll continue on your walk and explore little bits of the area each day.

1. The College Campus
Don't Miss:

- Old, ivy-trimmed buildings. Go inside and look at the marble floors, painted ceilings, carved moldings, dark wood. Look for the stone gargoyles in the stone window trim.
- Large, old homes. Notice the carved gingerbread wood trim, pastel colors, beveled glass, and Greek letters!
- Grassy Commons. Watch for street performers, soap-box politicians, "street characters" and students with outlandish dress.
- Carolinian towers. Climb up to the top. Stop and listen to the chiming of the hour.
- Performing Arts Building. Scan the art exhibits and photos of actors. Walk up and down ramps.
- University Museums. Take your pick: art, archeology, natural science, old books, old musical instruments. The collections are usually small enough to keep the kids interested.
- Ice Cream Parlours. Ask students which shop gives the largest scoops.
- Student restaurant hang-outs. The kids will love the pizza, burgers or submarine sandwiches. You'll be transported back to your college days.
- Student Unions. Read the posters, placards and graffitti. Buy a few university souvenirs.
- Outdoor Sculpture. Look for it. Almost every university campus offers examples of modern art, murals or monuments.

2. The Countryside
Don't Miss:

- Bridges. Look for the three billy goats gruff and the troll if you can walk across.
- Beaches. Feed the gulls, collect shells and plant life, draw designs on the wet sand using a twig.
- Lighthouses. Snoop around, climb up the stairs, look out to sea and pretend you see a ship in distress.
- Windmills. Watch. Listen to the wind. Take a picture at sunrise or sunset.
- Farms. Visit a petting farm, U-Pick fruit farm, demonstration farm. Buy fresh fruit and vegetables from a roadside stand and roam around the haystacks and crops.
- Mountains. Climb, collect rocks, look for fossils.
- Nature Trails. Look for Indian burial mounds, wild flowers, snakes and streams. Sing camp songs. Run around and be sure to follow the path markers!
- Cemetaries. Wander through respectfully, looking at dates of birth and death, and reading epitaphs. Talk about your ancestors, their births and deaths, invent stories about the people based on their tombstones.

3. The City

Don't Miss:

- Downtown Business Districts. Trace the jagged edges of the skyline. Take an outdoor elevator to the top of the tallest building. Count the number of brief cases and jogging shoes you see. Visit a money museum located inside a city bank.

- Wharfs and Marinas. Watch for street entertainers and street vendors. Tour old ships. Visit maritime museums. Read the names of all the pleasure crafts.

- Hotels. Wander around old and new hotel lobbies. Look for fountains, wall hangings, chandeliers. Visit the gift shops, ride the glass elevators.

- City/County Buildings. Visit libraries, court houses, post offices, capitol buildings. Look for beautiful marble, painted or tiled ceilings, carved moldings, domes. Look for historical paintings and sculpture.

- Museums. Take your pick: science and industry, natural science, natural history, aquarium, planetarium, art.

- Farmers' Market. Look for bunnies hiding under the tables laden with fresh produce. Soak in the smells and sounds. Buy a picnic lunch and pick up a few bargains in straw or craft ware.

- Window Shopping. Stop in converted old buildings. Point out art gallery, travel and airline windows. Watch for animated holiday windows.

- City Squares and Parks. Watch for artists, vendors and street entertainers. Take a carriage ride. Feed the pigeons gathered around monuments and sculpture.

- Factory Tours. Watch cars, cereal, baby foods, clothes, candy, tobacco or beer being made. Take home some free samples. Visit a winery and taste test the wines.

- Churches, Synagogues, Old Homes and Gardens. Notice the architectural details. Go inside and take the docent tour if it's short enough for the interest level of your kids. Wander around the gardens and gift shop.

RESTAURANT SURVIVAL GUIDE

Family vacations offer freedom from kitchen duty. Yet, eating three meals each day in a restaurant is not our idea of fun. Our kids are often restless, noisy and uncooperative. Sometimes they aren't even hungry, and tell us only after their deluxe taco arrives.

The best way to survive restaurant dining is finding alternatives to three meals out, remaining flexible and choosing your restaurants carefully.

If your family has a kitchenette, you'll enjoy casual breakfasts or light dinners in your accomodations. Remember not to take advantage of Mom. She's on vacation too.

NOTE TO MOM: Ahead of time tell the family what you're willing to do: breakfast every day, dinner twice, with help from the family, no lunches....

ALTERNATIVES

Reduce tension and food bills by eating only one or two meals daily in a restaurant.

Consider NOT GOING OUT FOR BREAKFAST...Instead:
- Order a room service breakfast to split with sleepy, cranky or slow-moving kids. You can nurse baby; the kids can eat while watching TV.
- Serve a picnic breakfast in the room. Kids love starting the day with cereal mini-packs, granola bars, crackers, cheese, fruit and cans of juice.
- Use Mom's and Dad's Early Morning Coping Kit and a few snacks to pacify everyone until you're ready for a mid-morning restaurant brunch.
- Start the day with a visit to the nearby bakery or croissant shop, and find an inviting spot for an outdoor picnic breakfast.

Consider NOT GOING OUT FOR LUNCH...Instead:

- Eat a big breakfast at a family restaurant and instead of lunch, have a middle of the day ice cream or other snack. Then eat an early dinner.
- Wander through the local deli and have every family member pick out a special item for a picnic lunch. Eat along the wharf.
- Carry-out fried chicken, pizza or other fast food and eat on the beach.
- Buy fruit and vegetables, cheese and dessert at the Farmers' Market. Eat at a city park.
- Have your hotel prepare you a box lunch. Eat in the car on the way to your next destination.

Consider NOT GOING OUT FOR DINNER...

Who says you must eat all your dinners in restaurants? If you've been on the go all day and the kids are tired, hungry and impaitent, why not enjoy the immediate gratification of a dinner picnic full of goodies and carry-outs, or the undemanding flexibility of a room service dinner?

HINT: If you are planning on a restful restaurant dinner, retire to your room in the late afternoon for quiet/nap time. You'll all wake up refreshed and rejuvenated, ready to dress for dinner and handle the wait.

CHOOSING RESTAURANTS

It's difficult being adventurous with hungry and impatient kids. That's why some families prefer eating only at fast food and family restaurant chains. They know what to expect and are rarely disappointed.

If you're willing to take risks, it's fun experimenting with local restaurants. Many times, we'll stop at a restaurant with a clever or cute sounding name, with an interesting awning or facade. Sometimes we close our eyes and pick a restaurant at random from the Yellow Pages.

Save yourself unexpected problems by calling ahead of time using the restaurant calling guide in this book or once there, read the menu before being seated. You can always leave and find a restaurant more suitable to your family's needs.

We've had good dining experiences in every type of restaurant, from fast foods to gourmet, family fare to ethnic cuisine.

We often know the minute we walk into a restaurant whether or not we'll have a good experience. The variables are usually the same:

- The restaurant is clean and attractive.
- You are seated quickly and the waitress offers the kids crackers or crayons.
- The kids have a difficult time deciding which of the kiddie menu items to choose. "Maybe we can come back tomorrow night and order the spaghetti," they mumble.
- The adult menu offers creative and nutritious sounding selections.
- Your service is fast; the food is hot and relatively tasty and...
- Best of all, there is enough noise to neutralize your family's noise.

Need we ask for more?

TIPS

1. Eat dinner before the crowds. You'll get better service before 6:00 and the kids will be able to satisfy their innate early dinner timer.

2. Read the menu while waiting in line so you can decide ahead of time what everyone should order.

3. When "reading" the menu to the kids, limit their choices.

4. Cut costs by ordering only water and asking for straws for each child.

5. Vary your seating arrangements from meal to meal. Try the buddy system, one child and one parent on each side of a booth. Sit between fighting siblings.

6. Specify where you'd like to be seated. For infants, use a booth, so the carseat will fit if he's sleeping. For toddlers, find a back room or a secluded area so his noise or movement won't distract other diners. Ask for "No Smoking" if you'll be more comfortable.

7. Keep the kids busy before the meal with their Restaurant Busy Kit.

8. If you forgot the Busy Kit (make a mental note to bring it along next time), play a few imagination games like "I Spy," "This Guy Has," or "Geography."

9. Ask the waitress for crackers or rolls. If the service is slow, walk over to the kitchen entrance and nicely ask the first available person for something to tide over the kids until their meal arrives.

10. Bring an extra high chair strap, scarf or belt to keep your child in the highchair. Usually the restaurant highchair's safety belt is broken.

11. Immediately upon sitting down, ask for extra napkins and remove from the table any dangerous or alluring items, such as matches, salt and pepper shakers, packets of sugar, knives, and glass ashtrays.

12. Feed infants right before leaving for the restaurant and they'll often oblige you by sleeping in their carseat on the bench of your booth.

13. Don't worry about nursing baby in the restaurant, provided you are being very discreet.

14. Try to make one potty stop with all the kids right before the food arrives.

15. Use the restaurant calling guide to be sure the restaurant meets your family's needs, before you walk a mile and realize what you thought was a family Chinese restaurant is really a fancy, reservations-only gourmet Chinese restaurant.

RESTAURANT CALLING GUIDE

Ask About:

• Reservations needed? suggested?

• Children's menu?

• Highchairs? Sassy seats? Boosters?

• Hours for breakfast, lunch, dinner?

• Buffet? Do children eat for ½ price or for free?

• Salad Bar?

• If fixed price, will child be charged if he isn't ordering any dinner?

• Non-smoking section?

• Is restaurant appropriate for children?

• Any vegetarian, fish, lo-calorie selections (or anything else you require)?

• Liquor license?

• Directions?

THE ORDERING GAME

We never win! When we split an order between the kids, they are suddenly ravenous and eat most of our meal, too. Then we're hungry and annoyed and swear next time we'll order a separate meal for each kid.

When we order separate meals for each kid—you guessed it—they suddenly lose their appetites and we are stuck with the guilt-inducing dilemma: DO WE WASTE FOOD OR EAT UP ALL THOSE EXTRA CALORIES?

Keep the family well-fed and happy by varying your ordering strategy.

Most kids like:

1. Eating soup as a main course and nibbling your crackers and the extra turkey from your salad.
2. Choosing items from the salad bar even though they'd never touch a salad at home.
3. Dressing elegantly and eating elegantly at a fancy restaurant—provided they're well-rested.
4. Making a meal out of rolls and butter. So don't order them too much else.
5. Having their own drinks. Order everyone water and have the waitress split the chocolate milk for two brothers in the kitchen.
6. Having their own plate. Ask for extra plates if you'll be sharing food.
7. Immediate gratification. If the kids are tired and very hungry, stick to fast foods or a buffet. You'll never enjoy your dinner otherwise.
8. Buffets. Just explain buffet etiquette: No pushing or shoving to spear the last olive. No hording the chocolate eclairs. It's okay to come back for more. It's okay to take only a little of everything to be sure you'll like it. It's important not to eat more than you can handle!
9. Pancake restaurants. Often the kids can eat the pancakes that come with your omelette.
10. Ethnic restaurants. Watching food prepared before their eyes is a special treat. They'll often eat foods if they are assured that what's inside is good and not weird. Ask for rolls if they still refuse to try the food.

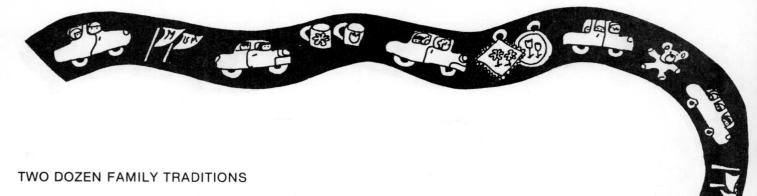

TWO DOZEN FAMILY TRADITIONS

Start a family tradition. Something you do on every vacation, no matter where you are. Something you collect as a family from every place you visit.

By comparing and collecting, the kids will begin to remember every trip and look forward to participating in the next family vacation tradition.

Family traditions can be as simple or elaborate as suits your style.

1. Attend a sporting event in every city.
2. Collect banners, cups, hats, scorebooks or t-shirts with local teams' emblems.
3. Experience every kind of transportation available:
   Trolley, subway, glass elevator, train, tram, bus, cab, boat, ferry, bicycle, covered wagon, carriage, pony, elevator, escalator, and moving ramp.
4. Taste your favorite ice cream flavor in every city.
5. Visit every local university campus.
6. Buy a university mug, banner, sticker, notebook or t-shirt.
7. Swim in every hotel's swimming pool.
8. Take a picture of the family next to the trusty car.
9. Mom or Dad—take turns sleeping with your kids.
10. Have a midnight snack.
11. Look up your last name in the phone book and count how many listings there are.
12. Have a picnic breakfast.
13. Try one new adventurous activity. Rent a boat, take a horsedrawn carriage, scuba dive, walk to the top of the tallest building.
14. Attend a local concert, play or puppet show.
15. Visit local libraries. Listen to tapes and records.
16. Buy a puppet from every spot.
17. Buy a book with pictures, photos or stories about every city.
18. Bring home fresh foods from the area: smoked fish, cherries, apple cider, fudge, chocolate.
19. Collect a special animal momento from every city. Have a family "mascot": unicorns, frogs, dogs, bunnies.
20. Go bowling on every trip.
21. Collect a t-shirt from every trip.
22. Collect pot holders or refrigerator magnets from every place.
23. Bring home canned and bottled local food to enjoy months later.
24. Act like a "Local" in every spot...

HOW TO ACT LIKE A LOCAL

When we stay in a new city, we like to get a feel for the native rhythms, flavors and people. We love acting like locals.

Here's how: First park the dead give-away, that overstuffed station wagon with its odd colored license plate, leave the camera behind, and thinly disguise your regional accent.

Now you're ready to cruise, and observe the native saunter, dialect and costume.

Try the following:

- Shop at a neighborhood grocery. Pick the funniest sounding local grocery chain or Ma and Pa shop. Lose your way in the "Pick Way" aisles and buy lots of treats at "Piggly Wiggly."
- Stop at the local truck stop or diner for a hearty meal and some colorful local gossip. Be sure to try the homemade specialities: pies, breads, soups.
- Walk into the town square for some nostalgic ice cream scooped and served at the soda counter.
- Cheer for the home team at a sporting event. Wear the team colors and outfit the kids in team hats to complete the disguise.
- Explore your new environment. Jog up and down residential streets, nod hello to real locals walking their dogs. Take the baby for a stroll down the big city's main thoroughfare. Subtly crane your neck up to see the highrises.
- Search out the local restaurant with authentic regional or ethnic foods. Close your eyes and try everything. Buy the kids a candy bar to go with their rolls if they balk at trying new foods.
- Catch up on the local news. Let the kids operate a newspaper vending machine. Check out the personalities of the local news anchors.
- Attend a worship service at a local church or synagogue. Compare the service structure with what you're used to. Talk to the congregants and notice the architectural work inside and outside the chapel.
- Play at the local park. Kids are naturals at forming an instant rapport with strangers their own size. In a few minutes, they will be quite involved in an imaginary sand box game with the miniature locals.
- Talk to the natives; they'll welcome your interest. In fact, the coffee shop waitress, pool lifeguard, subway seatmate and mothers at the park may be your best sources for inside information. Ask them where to eat, what to see, where to take the kids and what not to miss.

Problems

We hope you can skip this section and go on to the next but just in case you anticipate a problem or two, read on.

FINDING TREATMENT IN CASE OF ILLNESS OR INJURY*

*This is not a first aid manual, rather a guide to finding medical or dental care on a trip.

Kids aren't supposed to get sick on trips, right? We bring our trusty First Aid Kit just in case, ready to handle any minor illness, bumps and cuts.

Yet serious illness and injury is unpredictable and could happen anywhere. If Scott develops strep throat at a convention in Des Moines, or Jennifer chips a tooth at a Michigan ski resort, we need attention, fast.

How quickly and calmly we handle our children's illness or accidents might influence our vacation's outcome.

RULES TO REMEMBER

1. Be sure to have your hometown doctors' phone numbers with you. (Remember, the doctor will not give you a dignosis or a prescription over the phone, but will help with the child's medical history and advice.)
2. Carry a written list of all medicines your child is allergic to or has had a bad reaction to.
3. Carry a written list of all medicines family members are presently taking.
4. Carry your insurance company name and policy number.
5. If you work for a large company, carry the phone number of the corporate employee benefits office.
6. Don't expect to find a specialist in a small town or an out-of-the-way resort.
7. Most large medical centers or university hospitals will have a full staff of specialists and offer quality care.
8. Expect to pay for services rendered with a check, cash or credit card. Even if your insurance company covers your care, as an out-of-towner, you may be asked to pay and then be reimbursed from your insurance.
9. After business hours, you will probably need to find an Emergency Room or 24 hour Urgent Care Center.

IF YOUR CHILD IS SICK:

Check the Symptoms:
1. Take the child's temperature.
2. Ask a verbal child for symptoms (soreness, aches).
3. Use good judgement. Can the child continue at the family's present pace? Will over-the-counter remedies ease his discomfort? Or should you...

Find a Doctor:
1. Ask at the hotel desk if they have a hotel physician on call. Many large hotels do have a physician on 24 hour call.
2. If he cannot handle the problem, ask him for a referral to an area specialist.
3. Call friends or family in the area for a recommendation.
4. Call a large medical center or university hospital for a recommendation.
5. As a last resort, call the local Medical Society or look in the Yellow Pages.
6. If after hours, go to an Emergency Room, preferably located in a large medical center or university hospital. Or use a 24 hour Urgent Care Center or Immediate Care Center.

Stay Alert:
1. Ask about the doctor's credentials.
2. Explain that you are from out of town.
3. Ask the attending doctor to call your hometown doctor if you have questions about: allergy to medication, method of treatment, questionable diagnosis.
4. In an emergency room, ask to see a specialist if necessary.

IF YOUR CHILD HAS A RASH:

Check the Symptoms:
1. Take the child's temperature.
2. Ask a verbal child for symptoms. (Does it itch, burn, feel swollen?)
3. Examine the child to determine if the rash is in one localized area or is spreading.
4. If the symptoms are accompanied by a high or persistent fever or if the child is uncomfortable...

Find a Dermatologist or Pediatrician:
1. Ask the Hotel Physician for a referral.
2. Call friends or family in the area for a recommendation.
3. Call a large medical center or university hospital for a recommendation.
4. Check the phone book under Dermatology or Pediatrics, or call the local Medical Society.

IF YOUR CHILD IS INJURED:

Use good judgement:

1. Go to an Emergency Room, preferably affiliated with a large medical center or university hospital.
2. Ask for an Orthopedic Surgeon to look at a broken limb.
3. Ask for a Plastic Surgeon to look at a wound that requires stitches, especially if it is in a prominent place.
4. Be sure to make a follow up visit with your local doctor, once you return home.

IF YOUR CHILD'S TOOTH IS INJURED:

Use good judgement:

1. Look for excessive bleeding from the tooth.
2. Remember that trauma to the lip area can look worse than it is.
3. If bleeding persists after pressure is applied for several minutes, the child is still complaining and in pain, or if the tooth is broken and jagged...

Find a Dentist:

1. Call friends or family in the area for a recommendation.
2. Ask at the hotel desk for the name of a Pedodontist (Children's dentist)
3. Call the local Dental School for a recommenation.
4. Call the local Dental Society or look in the Yellow Pages.
5. After hours, call an Emergency Room. Some have dentists on call.

> CAUTION: If a permanent tooth is completely knocked out, it may be saved.
> Try this: Put the tooth in a jar of milk, salt water, or in a moist towel. Don't clean the tooth; you could destroy valuable tissue. Get to a dentist within 30 minutes. Time is a critical factor. An Endodontist would be the proper specialist, although a general dentist can treat this.

Misbehavior

We expect our kids to misbehave on trips, but when, where and how much always scares us. And what happens when everything crumbles and we start misbehaving too?

When we use our common sense, exercize flexibility and think in terms of alternatives, we may keep small problems from escalating into major catastrophes.

BEDTIME BLUES

IF THE CHILDREN WON'T SETTLE DOWN AND GO TO SLEEP...

Try:

1. A later bedtime.
2. A story or quiet activity.
3. A walk.
.4. Lights out and everyone (including parents) lies down. (This usually works within half an hour.)

CAUTION: Parents can fall asleep too, and awake with wide eyes at about 2:00 a.m., tiptoeing around a dark room and wondering what to do.

IF ONE CHILD IS SLEEPY AND EVERYONE ELSE IS READY FOR MORE FUN...

Try:

1. Letting the sleepy child go to sleep. The parent with the most reading material stays behind to babysit.
2. Encouraging the other parent to take the remaining children out for an evening stroll, swim, or snack.
3. Taking the sleepy child along for a walk in the stroller and hopefully, he'll fall asleep.

CAUTION: If he naps too long, he'll be ready for action when you're ready to go to sleep.

4. Taking the sleepy child with you to your next scheduled activity and encouraging him to go to sleep on your lap. (If tired enough, most five's and under will fall asleep anywhere.)

CAUTION: Understand that the sleepy child's misbehavior is a function of his fatigue.

5. Sharing a quiet activity in the room with the understanding that after, you'll all go out.

IF THE CHILDREN CONK OUT AT 8 PM EACH EVENING...AND ARE UP AT 6 AM EACH MORNING...

Try:

1. Keeping them out later one evening and insisting they sleep later the next morning. Hopefully, they'll adapt to a different sleep-wake schedule.

CAUTION: Some kids have seemingly inflexible internal alarm clocks. Be patient. With a little reprogramming, and a lot of understanding, they'll learn how to sleep later each morning to make up for a late night. Often, they become quite adept just in time for your return home.

2. Winding down in the afternoon for a short nap that will give the kids the energy needed to stay up later.
3. Adapting to their schedule. Turn in early yourself. You might as well catch up on your sleep. You'll need to face the kids at sunrise.
4. Putting the kids to bed on their side of the room and once they're asleep...taking advantage of time together with your spouse, quietly watching a movie, turning on the lights and reading, or pulling out the chocolate truffles you bought when the kids weren't looking.
5. Leaving the kids with a sitter.

CRYING BABIES

IF BABY CRIES AT A RESTAURANT...

Try:

1. Distracting him with a colorful toy, rattle or lovie.
2. Using a pacifier
3. Feeding him.
4. Holding him.
5. Taking him for a walk outside or in the lobby.
6. Changing his position in his seat.
7. Changing his diaper.
8. Re-thinking your restaurant choice.

HINT: If other diners look distraught, you're upset and your meal is rapidly becoming chaotic, you should stick to a family restaurant. At least in a family restaurant most diners have at one time or another been in the same circumstances as you. You can relax, do the best you can to distract baby and finish your meal at the table.

IF BABY CRIES LATE AT NIGHT OR EARLY MORNING...

Try:

1. Remaining calm.
2. Taking baby in bed with you to nurse or cuddle.
3. Feeding him an extra bottle.
4. Using a pacifier.
5. Rocking, pacing or walking him.
6. Singing, humming or playing with him.
7. Taking baby with you into the bathroom and turning on the fan.
8. Taking baby for a stroller walk.
9. Bathing baby.
10. Insisting on a nap for yourself the following day.

CAUTION: Sometimes, nothing works and baby just needs to have his cry. Allow him to let off a little steam and hope you won't bump into your hotel neighbor the next day.

ROWDY KIDS

IF THE KIDS ARE WILD...

They need:

1. More sleep.
2. A change of pace quiet activity. (Read a book, swim in the pool, write in your log)
3. A change of pace. Alternate a busy day with a quiet day. Take time out.
4. More input into daily decisions. Maybe they feel left out or angry?
5. Lots of run-around time or a physical activity.
6. Fewer sugary treats.
7. A meal. Maybe they are trying to tell you they are hungry?

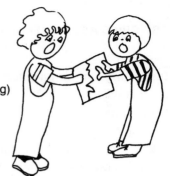

CAUTION: Have you ever noticed that yelling at or spanking rowdy kids usually quiets them for about four minutes, and then they resume, even louder?

IF THE KIDS ARE CRANKY...

They need:

1. More sleep.
2. More child-oriented activities.
3. More run-around time.
4. More hugs.
5. Fewer activities.
6. Less stimulation.
7. A chance to discuss their anger, fears, and frustrations.
8. Parents with a sense of humor and patience.

CAUTION: Try giving your "grouch" attention only when he is calm, not while he is cranky. Act casual. We've seen kids, who look like they were going to fall apart, do a complete turn around.

CRANKY PARENTS

IF YOU NEED TIME OUT...

Think of creative alternatives:
1. Grandma takes the kids out to dinner; Mom and Dad have a quiet dinner by themselves.
2. Mom takes the kids swimming; Dad takes a nap.
3. Dad takes the kids out for a meal; Mom orders in room service and finishes reading her book.
4. Dad visits his favorite museum; Mom meets an old friend for lunch and introduces her to the kids.

CAUTION: Too much family togetherness is not always productive or healthy. A short break for each parent will refresh and recharge the entire family relationship. Don't ''grin and bear it.'' Once you think creatively and take a break, you'll schedule time out on every trip.

IF YOU NEED TIME TO RELAX...

Schedule:
1. A children's activity where you can just observe. Watch the kids bowl, climb on playground equipment, or build cities in a sandbox.
2. A movie. Mom and Dad can take turns dozing off while the kids enjoy a movie and popcorn.
3. A visit to the local gift shop. Let the kids buy an inexpensive toy. Go back to the hotel room for play time. Mom and Dad can rest or read.

IF YOU NEED PRIVATE TIME...

Check out:

1. Your hotel's supervised daytime children's activities. Request that the kids have a one hour trial run. Tell the staff your intention. They'll probably show the kids a great time.
2. Your hotel's babysitting services.

CAUTION: Inviting a stranger to care for your kids is a risk. Recognize this fact and make careful decisions.

•We feel more comfortable leaving a babysitter with two or more verbal children.

•Always use a sitter referred by the hotel.

•Ask for credentials, experience and age.

•Have the sitter arrive 30 minutes early so you can visit and introduce the kids.

•Don't leave if you don't feel comfortable with the sitter.

•If you feel a little uneasy, don't go far away. Enjoy a dinner in the hotel restaurant.

•Don't expect a young child who doesn't separate easily at home to do well with a stranger in a strange place.

•Don't consider babysitters if you're not comfortable with the idea. Instead...

Consider Alternatives:

1. Spend extra money for a suite of two rooms or adjoining rooms. You will have greater flexibility when the kids go to sleep.
2. Make the best of stolen moments, when the kids are occupied or asleep.
3. Make plans to take a trip without the kids soon after your return. Just thinking about this should tide you over all the rough spots!

Getting Home

Reorganizing

REORGANIZING

In some ways, returning home from a vacation is like knowing the end of a good movie. There is no punch line, no excitement, no anticipation.

We put ourselves in reverse, repacking, pulling out the travel games and regathering our ingenuity and patience in order to face the long ride home.

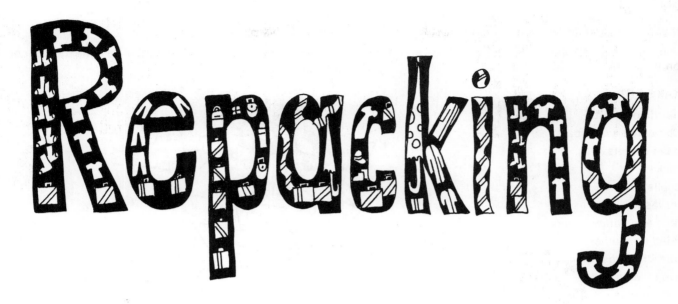

Repacking

We can't avoid it. We've got to repack our belongings and fit them back into the car. This is the part of the trip we dread. Our clothes have grown during this trip; our possessions have doubled. We have misplaced the house keys and the kids have two clean socks between them, one blue and one white.

Someone has to get it all together! Take it from parents with experience, repacking in an organized fashion will save time and effort once home.

So supress your natural desire to STUFF everything back into the suitcase in a haphazard way. Remember, it takes about 275 hours to unstuff and organize vacation belongings packed in complete disarray. Some belongings have even been known to permanently disappear.

HINT: Keep in mind the reality of Monday morning. Will the kids go to school without underwear? Will you find your deodorant and electric shaver? Will the family have anything clean to wear?

A REPACKING STRATEGY

SEARCH

Create a team of searchers and assign areas. Young children like to look under beds. Older children willingly open and close every dresser drawer. Shake out the bed linens and towels; look inside closets and behind doors. Stray socks, a toothbrush, a stuffed bear, a pajama top and a box of crayons are usually our families' booty.

One family, who left in a hurry without a thorough search party was surprised to find a large package at the front door when they arrived home. It was one abandoned, matted, stuffed dog, sent home C.O.D. The postage cost as much as the dog!

SEPARATE

For compulsives and those ready to clean up their act, we suggest keeping dirty clothes separate from the clean, right from the beginning of the trip. Use garbage bags, duffles, large plastic bags, or pillow cases. Designate one—DARKS, one—LIGHTS OR WHITES, and one—HEAVILY SPOTTED.

Keeping the dirty clothes separate will give you an accurate view of the number of clean clothes left for each family member. You will also be free from the messy task of separating gooey and sandy clothes. The laundry will seem a contained and tamed animal, not the growling, growing, overwhelming beast brought home on past trips.

HINT: If your suitcases are almost empty, combine everyone's clean clothes into one suitcase and place dirty laundry bags inside the other suitcases. Mark the luggage so you'll know which suitcases to open near the washing machine and which to carry right into the bedroom.

SELECT

If your kids are like ours, they've collected something new every day of the trip.

Thin out the possessions of their duffle bags and Busy Kits. (You know your own kids. Should this be done together or on the sly?)

TAKE OUT:

petrified donuts

half eaten candy bars

dead insects

rocks

shells

leaves

gum and candy wrappers

dried up markers

torn drawings

live insects

broken toys

SHOULD YOU THROW THESE TREASURES OUT? WE LEAVE THAT MORAL DECISION TO YOU.

REORGANIZE:

Put the crayons back into their box.

Place the caps back on the markers.

Smooth out the paper.

Find the doll's head.

Put the games back together.

Put the rubberband on the baseball cards.

HIDE:

Place securely in the suitcase any new toys that will not be safe in the car. Frisbees, magic balls, boomerangs, and paper airplanes will be fun once home. Don't fall for the "I'll just hold it" routine.

O.K. So you're driving home. Don't just put the car into automatic pilot and forget about having fun. Remember what an adventure you had getting there?

Repeat after us, "The trip isn't over yet." With a little creative planning and left over impulsiveness, the return home can be as exciting and memorable a family adventure as the trip there.

PLANNING TIPS

GET EVERYONE INVOLVED...

- Pull out the maps and tourbooks. Trace an alternate route home. The scenic route. The plantation route. The coastal route. Drive through your ancestral home town. Visit Grandma and Grandpa, your best friend from high school, your brother's old girl friend.
- Visit the local grocery and let each child choose one or two snacks for the ride home.
- Decide as a family where and when you'll eat your meals. A roadside inn? Country park? Rest stop picnic area? Favorite fast food restaurant? Famous area restaurant?

CONTINUE EXPLORING...

- Stop at a special sight along the way: parks, wineries, house tours, factories, theme parks.
- Break up a long drive home into a special overnight stop midway.

MAKE THE FUN LAST...

- Save favorite activities, games, tapes and toys for the ride home. Be sure you haven't packed away all necessary "lovies."
- Stop for dinner close to home at the family's favorite home town restaurant.
- Pick up a carry-out dinner and eat it on paper plates, once home.

ACTIVITIES FOR THE ROAD HOME

Driving home activities should be enjoyable pastimes. They can also ease the entire family from a vacation mindset into a "home sweet home" mindset.

Help your family get ready for the shock of returning home. Use your time in the car constructively. Discuss the trip, plan new family activities, and visualize what your life will be like once you return.

1. Ask children to picture their bedrooms. Ask them specific questions: What toys do you miss the most? Which sheets are on your bed? What stuffed animals are waiting for you? What color is your carpet?

2. Ask children to visualize their home. Ask them: What room or special area of the house do you miss the most? What will you see first when we open the door? What do you think will look different? What do you think we will find in the refrigerator? In the pantry? In the garden? In the yard?

3. Ask children to make a list of things to do when they return home. Call Emily...Write a thank you to Aunt Judy...Unpack my Busy Kit...Finish my homework...Feed my goldfish.

4. Make a shopping list of foods to buy once home. Let the kids talk about their favorite school lunches, snacks, and what they really missed during their trip.

5. Ask each family member to name something he's looking forward to doing once home. Go around the car in round robin fashion. This is a great activity for the family that begins feeling sad and tense as the car moves closer to home.

6. Reread your daily log. Talk about your adventures and misadventures.

7. Play trip trivia, using your log. Ask children the names of places, restaurants and people. What did the lifeguard look like? What was the name of the parrot in the hotel lobby? What color was Aunt Diane's car?

8. Pretend you are traveling a magic road that leads to a secret and exotic place. Take turns telling stories about this special destination.

9. Plan special family activities and time together for the next few weeks.
A family picnic...A family bike ride...Dinner together at Grandma's...A trip to the library...A family walk.

10. Plan a future family trip. Where would the kids like to go? Who should we visit? When should we go? This is a good time to talk about the cost of travel and the meaning of the word, "maybe."

11. If the kids are occupied or sleeping, plan a "parents only" vacation. Even one night away is refreshing.

12. Plan the dinners for the first week home designating each family member, "Chef for the Day." Let the Chef decide on dessert, main course and vegetable for his meal. Make a list and post it on the refrigerator, once home.

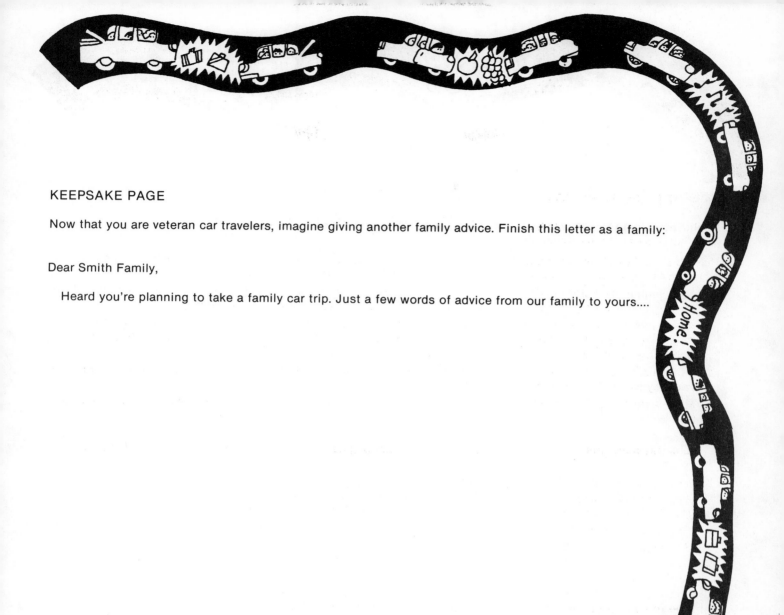

KEEPSAKE PAGE

Now that you are veteran car travelers, imagine giving another family advice. Finish this letter as a family:

Dear Smith Family,

   Heard you're planning to take a family car trip. Just a few words of advice from our family to yours....

KEEPSAKE PAGE

Imagine returning to your vacation spot. Write down each family member's quotable quote.

The next time I visit, I will...

The next time I visit, I'll never...

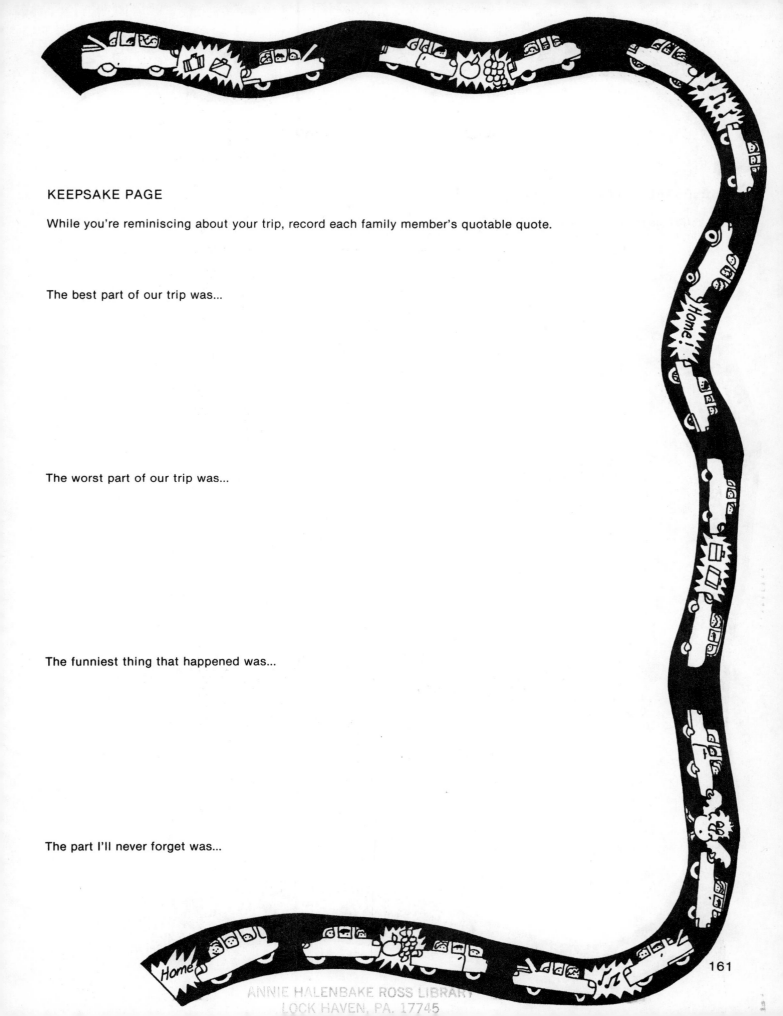

KEEPSAKE PAGE

While you're reminiscing about your trip, record each family member's quotable quote.

The best part of our trip was...

The worst part of our trip was...

The funniest thing that happened was...

The part I'll never forget was...

161

KEEPSAKE COLORING PAGE

Ask the kids to draw themselves at their favorite spot or doing their favorite trip activity. Have them give their drawing a title, too.

Note: A child may draw in the space provided—or draw on separate sheets of paper (especially if there are siblings.) Staple or tape the drawings to this page.

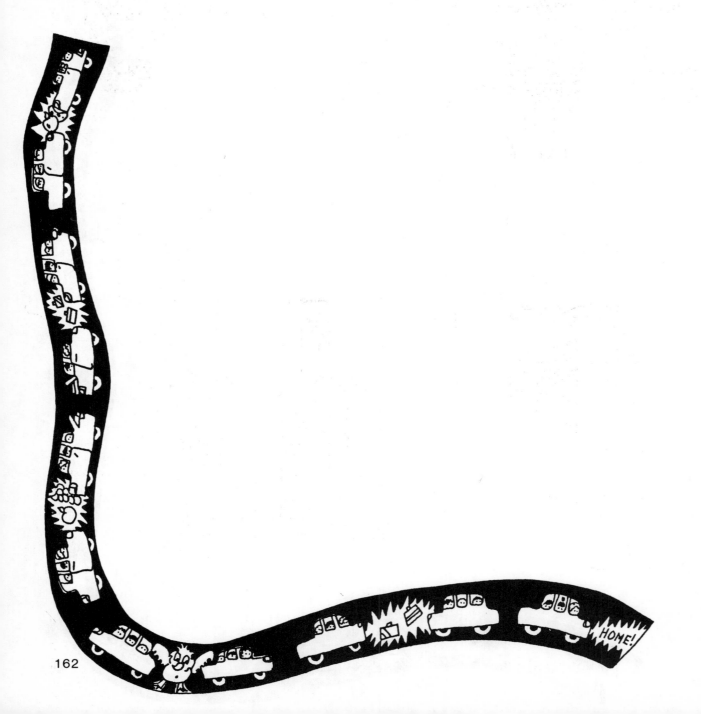

REENTERING

We approach home with dread, thinking of all the responsibilities lying in wait for us.

We arrive home exhausted, the kids whining and fighting. The grass needs to be cut, the mail must be read, the clothes have to be washed.

We are in the grips of Coming Home Anxiety.

Why did we ever go away?

Coming Home Anxiety is real. Those of us who suffer from it are easy to identify. Once friendly, exuberant and fun loving, we experience a metamorphosis on the road home.

First it's a feeling of tightness, right around the throat and stomach, as we flash across our conscience all the responsibilities we set aside until after the trip. Next, the feeling of overwhelming guilt as we mentally tally all the calories we consumed. We are unable to concentrate, to make simple decisions. We snap at the kids and at innocent by-standers.

Minutes from home we experience overwhelming confusion, tension, and exaggerated anxiety. What if the house burned down? What if robbers broke in and found our secret candy lair? What if our answering machine broke? The basement flooded?

We picture soggy newspapers piled next to the front door, snow so deep we can't even drive up to the garage, our neighbor's weeds relocated on our lawn.

There is no cure for Coming Home Anxiety. Hopefully, you've planned to take an extra day off work to reorganize your life. And remember, a slow but sure schedule will get you through.

HOME SWEET HOME

The house is still standing and it seems like we never left. The basketball still sits in the flowerbed; the peonies are still in bloom; the hedge still needs cutting.

The neighborhood kids run to greet us as we pull into the driveway. Our kids jump out, anxious to be back on their own turf, free to wander and yell, without restraint.

Home sweet home. Our own cozy beds, our clean clothes (at least what's left lying in the bottom of our drawers), our own washer and dryer, our own space.

Back to normal...back to our old routine...back to the pressing needs of work and home.

Oh, those pressing needs...

Where's the food?

- Stop at the neighborhood shop on the way home to buy the essentials.
- Defrost supplies from the freezer and use your microwave.
- Ask a friend or relative to stock your refrigerator the day before your return.
- Eat the first meal back at Grandma's or a fast food spot and wait until tomorrow to go grocery shopping.

Where's the washing machine?

- Dig in. It's got to be done.
- Separate and wash those clothes you'll need immediately.
- Let the kids fold and put away their own clothes.
- Push to the side and ignore whatever clothes you'll wash tomorrow.

Where's Spot?

- We know you're anxious to see him, but do everyone a favor, keep him in the kennel one more day.
- You'll be able to devote more time to Spot once things have calmed down.

Where's the car?

- Clean up the car before stray animals take up residence.
- Place the kids in charge of their own bags, toys, pillows, and odds and ends.
- Have a contest. Give each kid a garbage bag and see who can fill it up with trash first.

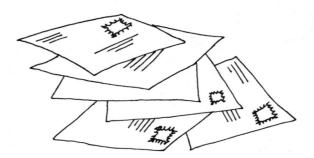

Where's the mail?

- Be sure you're home when the mail is delivered. It probably won't fit into the mailbox.
- Separate into piles: mine, yours, theirs, read immediately, toss out, put away for next week.
- Be careful. We've buried bills and invitations between circulars.

Who's there?

- Try to keep a low profile for at least one day.
- Check in with important people, but tell them you'll call back soon for a lengthy description of your trip. They'll understand.
- Discourage the kids from inviting over friends the first few days back.

What's this?

- Find a big box or envelope and stash all the souvenirs, tourbooks, maps and momentos until you have the time and desire to go through them.

Where's the bed?

- Change baby and toddler into their pj's at your last stop.
- Keep important sleep paraphernalia packed together and easy to find.
- Give older kids a chance to unwind and enjoy their toys and room again before bedtime.

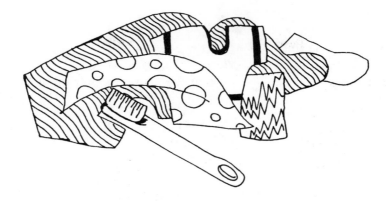

Where's my toothbrush?

• Told you not to stuff everything back indiscriminately into the suitcase!

Where's my datebook? Where's my life?

• Relax. Everything will get done, eventually.
• Make a list of all the tasks, phone calls and errands necessary to take your life off hold.
• Give yourself at least a week, or more, to feel caught up and back to normal.

HINTS: Most kids are happy to be home and playing with their toys in familiar surroundings. They will probably let you work without interruption.

              Maybe Grandma and Grandpa will be so lonely, they'll pick up the kids and give you a few free hours.

              Some families like to share tasks. Make your list in the car on the way home. Have each family member choose a task to complete before school or work begins.

POST VACATION BLUES

Even those family members most anxious to return find themselves moody and upset once home. For a variety of reasons, it's quite natural to feel tense and stressed after vacation.

REASON #1. REENTRY TAKES ENERGY

You've plunged back into the real world of responsiblity, demands, commitments and deadlines. You will need as much reserve strength, patience and motivation as you can muster to survive your first week back.

So...

- **Don't come home overtired!** Consciously go to bed as early as possible the last few nights of the trip.
- **Don't stay up late trying to accomplish everything the first day back!** Let the list wait. Take a walk, a bath, read a book, go to sleep.
- **Don't come back at the last possible moment!** Give yourself at least one full day as a buffer to sleep, rest, and reorganize yourself before returning to work.
- **Don't expect your spouse to comfortably take on all parenting responsibilities after sharing them during the trip!** Discuss the issue and agree on what expectations are realistic.
- **Don't ignore your date book or calendar!** Be aware of the upcoming week's events and activities so you can anticipate and meet the needs of each situation.
- **Don't play the martyr!** Just because you had a week of freedom, you don't have to repent by working extra hard. Schedule a special activity so you have something exciting to look forward to the first week: lunch with a friend, dinner with your spouse, starting a new book, going to see a movie.

• **Don't forget to ask for help!** Take shortcuts. Order in dinners, let the kids buy lunch, buy the cookies for the Brownie meeting instead of baking.
Hire babysitters to give you time for errands.

REASON #2. RECAPTURING TAKES PLANNING

The car pulls into the garage and everyone breaks into tears. The week of family togetherness is over. On Monday, Mom and Dad go back to work; the kids go back to daycare, school or camp. The rush of daily activities gives us little time for family togetherness and shared experience.

Why give up that cozy sense of family harmony? Nurture it throughout the year by building into each week special family time.

FAMILY TIME

1. Come together as a family and make a list of activities you like to do together.
2. Try to include activities that suit the wide range of family interests and ages.
3. Start small and try to be consistent.
4. Often the best activities take place around the house and cost very little.

Try:

SING-A-LONGS. Take turns selecting a song everyone knows or one with a repetitive chorus that is easy to learn.

MEALS. Take turns planning menus and innovative meal themes. Teach everyone how to use chopsticks. Have a picnic indoors.

BAKING. Look through cookbooks and find recipes that are easy to manage. Give the kids aprons and let them help you make dessert.

MYSTERY DRIVES. Surprise the kids. Tell them to hop in the car and don't tell them where you are going. End up at an ice cream parlor, a park, a friend's house, or go feed the neighborhood ducks.

CLUBS. Start a family club that meets on your bed, under the covers on Sunday morning. Play tickling games and make up funny words.

HOBBIES. Join each other in an enjoyable task. Build a birdhouse. Start a rock collection. Plant a vegetable garden. The trick is to get everyone involved at his own ability level.

SPORTS. After dinner, play baseball, basketball or soccer. Challenge the younger kids to a game of hide and seek or tag.

STROLLS. Walk around the block together. Pull the younger kids in a wagon. Collect twigs, rocks or leaves.

STORY HOURS. Curl up together, read aloud or create your own adventures.

REASON #3. RE-EVALUATION TAKES GUTS

We tossed our limits and rules to the wind for the sake of sanity. We slept in one hotel room, kept the kids up late and ate ice cream every day. Now we're home and we expect everyone to return to his usual routine. It's not so easy!

Just try:

- Explaining to Baby he can no longer sleep in the same room with you and won't be able to wake in the middle of the night for an extra feeding and special song.
- Forcing your six and ten-year-old into bed at 8:00 when they're used to watching the late night news.
- Telling three sisters they must sleep in their own separate beds when they're used to pillow fights and snuggling up to one another.

The kids will...

...object to greenbeans and eggplant when they've subsisted on french fries, hamburgers and hotdogs.

...be conditioned to think "food" every time they get into the car.

...forget you aren't a short order cook and demand pancakes, waffles, hot cereal and eggs for breakfast.

...expect souvenirs from the local grocery store, drugstore and every other place you take them into.

...demand all sorts of attention if you visited Grandma and Grandpa.

PLAN YOUR COURSE OF ACTION.

You know your child best. Either jump right in and consistently follow your at home rules, or gently ease into your routine, knowing it may take a few weeks.

BE PREPARED FOR A TRANSITION.

Whatever you decide to do, expect your kids to bargain, fight, throw tantrums and generally, be upset and moody. This is a stressful time for them, too.

KIDS ARE ADAPTABLE:

They will usually readapt their sleeping, eating and behavior patterns within a week. Try to remain good natured and follow through with your requests and rules.

If you begin feeling frustrated, think about the fun and togetherness of the trip. Remember, part of your annoyance with the kids may stem from your own return to the pressures of work and chores.

Remembering

You shot ten rolls of movie film, snapped five rolls of photographs and gathered piles of pamphlets, placemats, paper umbrellas and postcards. The kids collected stray rocks, plastic toothpicks and several souvenirs that could self destruct at any moment.

What can you do with all these vacation collectables?

TRANSFORM MOMENTOS INTO KEEPSAKES

1. Create a photo montage of your trip. Buy a large, clear plastic picture frame, and cut light weight poster board to fit the frame. Have fun with your pile of photographs by cutting around heads and bodies. Mount these photos to the cardboard using double sided masking tape or looped cellophane tape. Try to fill the cardboard with photos so the background color doesn't show.

2. Complete the ultimate photo album with quotable quotes. Mount your photos in the album. Cut out shapes and write funny dialogue. Attach these dialogue balloons to the photographs with looped cellophane tape.

3. Store your photos in an album with plastic slots the exact size of your particular film size. Before sliding them into the slots, label them with dates, places and names. Or attach a sticker every few pages with the dates and places written out.

4. Start a scrapbook, either individually for each child, or one for the entire family. Glue in everything that will lie flat. Write comments on each page explaining each item's significance.

LET THE KIDS GET IN ON THE ACT

1. Let each child select several photos to put up in his room. Encourage him to write a story, poem or letter about the photo.

2. Give the kids a pile of pamphlets and maps. Encourage their play. They can pretend to be a travel agent, or pretend to take their dolls or animals on a trip.

3. Offer kids the opportunity to write and illustrate a book about their trip. Remind them this can be real or imaginary. Have plenty of white paper, crayons and markers. Use construction paper for covers. Make sure your stapler is full.

PLAN AN EVENING OF SHOW AND TELL

1. Invite grandparents or very close friends over to view your home movies. Give each family member the chance to narrate. Keep it short! (For a longer version, do a family-only version.)

2. Have each family member show the souvenirs he bought and explain why they appealed to him.

3. Play a game of family trivia with your photographs. Who can remember the name of the street we're standing on? What day of the week was this photo taken? What did everyone eat for lunch at this restaurant?

4. Put photographs in a shoe box. Each family member pulls out a picture and gives it a funny, serious or fanciful title.

HELP YOUR KIDS REMEMBER FRIENDS AND FAMILY

1. Start a correspondance with the family and friends you visited. Now your kids can have a pen pal in another state. Address the envelopes for small children and let them put inside special drawings and small flat toys.

2. Keep a list of "Things to tell Grandma" near the phone and encourage the kids to add their ideas. When grandparents call, you can refer to the list and encourage the kids to talk about these topics.

3. Start a scrapbook of "My Family" and include photos of all out-of-town family members. Encourage the kids to leaf through often and talk about each relative and what they remember most about that person.

INDEX